CALIFORNIA SPORTS TRIVIA

Raul Guisado
and
J. Alexander Poulton

2011 by OverTime Books
First printed in 2011 10 9 8 7 6 5 4 3 2 1
Printed in Canada

All rights reserved. No part of this work covered by the copyrights hereon may be reproduced or used in any form or by any means—graphic, electronic or mechanical—without the prior written permission of the publisher, except for reviewers, who may quote brief passages. Any request for photocopying, recording, taping or storage on information retrieval systems of any part of this work shall be directed in writing to the publisher.

The Publisher: OverTime Books is an imprint of Éditions de la Montagne Verte

Library and Archives Canada Cataloguing in Publication

Guisado, Raul, 1971–
    California sports trivia / Raul Guisado, J. Alexander Poulton.

ISBN 978-1-897277-61-4

    1. Sports—California—Miscellanea. I. Poulton, J. Alexander (Jay Alexander), 1977– II. Title.

GV584.C2G85 2011   796.09794   C2010-907612-5

Project Director: J. Alexander Poulton
Editor: Jordan Allan
Cover Image: Skateboarder: ©Jupiterimages; surfer: © Ablestock; dragster: © 2010 Igor Lubnevskiy / Thinkstock; McAfee Oakland Coliseum: © 2008 permanently scatterbrained / Eric Molina; Candlestick Park: © 2008 cho_kettie / Marc Choquette, CC–Creative Commons; track sprinter: © Jupiterimages; speedboat: © Joe Stone | Dreamstime.com; golfer: © iStockphoto.com/Sergey Kashkin; football: © Toddtaulman | Dreamstime.com; baseball glove: © Bobbiholmes | Dreamstime.com; boxing gloves: © Zedcor Wholly Owned; all other images: © Photos.com.

We acknowledge the financial support of the Government of Canada through the Book Publishing Industry Development Program (BPIDP) for our publishing activities.

 Canadian Heritage   Patrimoine canadien

PC: 1

Table of Contents

Introduction 6

Chapter 1:
Golden State Gridiron 8

Chapter 2:
Hardball Cali-Style 56

Chapter 3:
California Hoops 91

Chapter 4:
Hockey in California? 106

Chapter 5:
Beautiful Game, Beautiful State 124

Chapter 6:
Country Club Livin' 127

Chapter 7:
Life's a Beach in California 136

Chapter 8:
CA = Action Sports Mecca 156

Chapter 9:
Endurable Californians 172

Chapter 10:
Golden State Sun AND Snow 186

Chapter 11:
But Wait, There's More! 190

Notes on Sources 206

Dedication

For Kendra and Dylan, my supportive and amazing wife and son

– Raul Guisado

For Claudette and Jeff

– J. Alexander Poulton

Acknowledgments

Sports have been an important part of my personal life from a young age, and I am a strong believer in the power that sports have to both transform and enrich our lives on so many levels. I feel very fortunate thus far to have been able to make sports the focus of my professional life and am appreciative of the opportunity to be involved in this project. Most importantly, I'd like to give huge thanks to the team at OverTime Books for their tremendous work. It was truly a pleasure to work with them.

– Raul Guisado

Introduction

California is a large and beautiful state with a diverse population and a varied geography—and contrary to popular belief, it's not just one giant beach. Enthusiasts and über-fanatics of just about any sport you can think of can be found somewhere in California. Some would say that trivia is the life and breath of sports, and a wide array of sports and their key figures have become an important part of the California way of life as well as the state's history.

"The Golden State" is the third largest state in the United States, behind Alaska and Texas, and is 770 miles long and 250 miles wide at its most distant points. California has 840 miles of general coastline on one side and is bordered by two mountain ranges—the Cascade Mountains and the Sierra Nevada. California is also home to the lowest point in the United States (Death Valley at 282 feet below sea level) and the highest point in the contiguous 48 states (Mt. Whitney at 14,494 feet).

This variety in climate and terrain, along with a diverse population of nearly 39 million, means that virtually every sport—team, water, indoor, outdoor, individual, mountain, air, motor, combat, action, endurance and "other" sport on the planet—is being passionately pursued somewhere in California. And the Golden State is home to 20 major professional sports franchises, more than any other U.S. state.

As much as they all deserve to be covered, this *California Sports Trivia* book focuses on the sports that are the most popular throughout the state. So sit back, relax and enjoy some sports trivia that is not so trivial to the California lifestyle and the history of sports worldwide.

Chapter One

Golden State Gridiron

San Francisco 49ers

The Catch

I don't need to tell any hardcore San Francisco 49er fans the meaning of "The Catch," but for those who might be unaware of the story and its significance, the play in question ranks as one of the most memorable events in the history of the National Football League (NFL).

The whole story began when the Dallas Cowboys and the San Francisco 49ers faced off in the 1982 NFC championship game for the chance to move on to the Super Bowl. The 49ers had a slightly better regular season record than the Cowboys, but the two squads were evenly matched in terms of skill in defense and offense. Hype prior to the start of the game had sports writers predicting a close, hard-fought game, and they were right.

San Francisco opened up the scoring in the first quarter with an eight-yard touchdown pass by Joe Montana to wide receiver Freddie Solomon. The 49ers could not hold on to the lead for long as the Cowboys roared back on the next possession and scored a 44-yard field goal, and then a 26-yard touchdown reception put Dallas in the lead 10–7 by the end of the quarter.

In the second quarter, the 49ers again took back the lead thanks to another sweet Joe Montana pass to make the score 14–10. But then three plays later, the Cowboys came right back when running back Tony Dorsett crossed the line, putting Dallas back on top 17–14 at halftime.

As the sports writers had predicted, the game exchanged leaders until Dallas pulled ahead late in the game by a score of 27–21 in the dying moments of the fourth quarter. It hardly seemed possible that the 49ers could make a comeback given the Cowboys' tight defense, but when you have Joe Montana on your side, anything is possible.

Montana to Clark

With just 4:54 left on the clock, the 49ers were on their own 11-yard line and faced with the daunting task of battling down the field. Montana played the field with surgical precision and managed to carry his team 89 yards, right down to the Cowboys six-yard line. Faced with a third down and three yards to go with only 58 seconds left on the clock, Joe Montana absolutely *had* to make the next play or their season was over.

Montana called the play, took the snap and looked for wide receiver Freddie Solomon, but the Cowboys had anticipated the move and covered the receiver perfectly. In the confusion of the play, the Cowboys broke through the 49ers' offensive line and pushed

Montana back toward the sideline, their sights on a sack. But without a moment to spare, Montana pump faked to Ed "Too Tall" Jones and then threw a high pass to the back of the end zone. As the ball soared over the heads of the Cowboys defense, it looked like the pass was headed directly out of bounds, when suddenly 49ers receiver Dwight Clark appeared out of nowhere and made a leaping grab, just managing to catch the ball with the tips of his fingers for the go-ahead touchdown with just 51 seconds left in the game, making the score 28–27 for the 49ers.

The called play, named "Red Right Tight–Sprint Right Option," marked both Solomon and Clark as the intended receivers. If all had gone according to plan, Montana was supposed to roll to his right and find an open Solomon. For Clark, the play called for him to cut across left, then immediately stop and head back to the right for the reception pass. Montana was supposed to be able to see the open target in Clark's mid-section, but because of the pressure by the Cowboys' defense, the pass was high, leaving it to Clark to make the spectacular catch.

But with 51 seconds left, the Cowboys still had a chance to get the ball within field goal–striking distance. The Cowboys' quarterback, Danny White, stepped up to the pressure and threw a complete pass to Drew Pearson that nearly ended with a touchdown, but 49ers defensive back Eric Wright made the tackle to stop the advance. Two plays later, 49ers' defensive end Lawrence Pillers sacked Danny White, forcing a fumble that was recovered by 49ers linesman Jim Stuckey, ending the game.

Post Catch

After the game, there was speculation that Montana had not intended to hit Clark with the end zone pass and was merely trying to throw the ball away because of the pressure and go for the touchdown on the fourth down. Montana was the first to refute this claim. Though he could not see the end zone, he said he knew Clark would be where he was supposed to be and simply made the blind pass.

"I saw Dwight's feet touch the ground. I heard the crowd scream," said Montana after the game.

The 49ers head coach Bill Walsh saw the ball sailing high and assumed that it would miss the mark and sail out of bounds, so he immediately began to plan for the fourth down until the roar of the crowd signaled the successful touchdown.

The 49ers advanced to the Super Bowl and eventually won the franchise's first championship title. The 49ers then went on to dominate the '80s, winning four Super Bowls and making the playoffs in 8 out of 10 seasons, while the Cowboys slipped out of contention and had to wait until the 1990s before they became a team to be reckoned with again.

An image of the catch, captured by photographer Walter Looss Jr., graced the cover of *Sports Illustrated* the following week. "The Catch" remains an iconic play, not just in San Francisco 49ers' history, but also for the entire NFL. Dwight Clark and Joe Montana re-enacted "The Catch" on its 25th anniversary on

November 5, 2006, at Candlestick Park during halftime at a 49ers–Minnesota Vikings game.

> *It's humbling really. I feel honored people are still talking about it, 25 years later. I am honored to be able to be a part of a play that was kind of the culmination of just this incredible surprise season. It's great to give 49er fans that moment that they can relive over and over and over, and I know they do because when I am in San Francisco and a lot of places, people want to talk about that play and how it crushed the Cowboys and sent them into submission for a decade. I never get tired of talking about it; I never get tired of seeing it, because I sign pictures and send them to people. I see that catch every day. I may sit and think about that moment a couple of times a year, and how awesome it was to be a part of that play and to be a part of the 49ers in the '80s!*
>
> –Dwight Clark

Team History

The 49ers first began as an All-America Football Conference (AAFC) team at the end of World War II. The first owners were Anthony J. "Tony" Morabito, his younger brother, Victor, and partners in the Lumber Terminals of San Francisco, Allen E. Sorrell and E.J. Turre. The team was named in honor of the miners who had come out west during the 1849 Gold Rush. In 1950, the AAFC went belly up and San Francisco, Baltimore and Cleveland were all awarded franchises in the NFL. The San Francisco 49ers became the first major league professional sports franchise to be based in San Francisco.

The DeBartolo Family

Edward John DeBartolo Sr., born in 1909, is considered the father of the American shopping mall. In 1971, the Edward J. DeBartolo corporation, based in Ohio, was ranked 47th in the nation for construction contractors. In 1983, DeBartolo made it onto the *Forbes* magazine list of "richest Americans." He bought the San Francisco 49ers franchise in 1977 and gave the team to his son, Edward J. DeBartolo Jr.

Eddie DeBartolo Jr. developed shopping malls for his father's company and helped it become one of the largest public real estate companies in the United States. At one point, the corporation owned over two billion square feet of retail space around the country. Eddie DeBartolo Jr. is considered by many to be one of the greatest owners in NFL history. He put a lot of effort into the 49ers and made them the most successful NFL franchise of the 1980s.

DeBartolo was actively involved in the team and some attribute the success of the 49ers to be, at least in part, a result of him being one of the most generous owners in professional sports. Over the 23 years that he owned the team, San Francisco won an unprecedented five Super Bowls (XVI, XIX, XXIII, XXIV and XXIX).

The five Super Bowl wins from 1982 to 1994, along with several other stellar seasons during the 1980s and 1990s, made the 49ers a dominant force in the NFL. They have earned a spot in football history as one of the most successful teams of those two decades and were the first franchise to win five Super Bowls.

However, DeBartolo's ownership of the 49ers was cut a little shorter than he anticipated as a result of his involvement in the corruption case of former Louisiana governor Edwin Edwards. In 1998, the federal government indicted Edwards for extortion and other charges. Apparently, he demanded $400,000 from DeBartolo in exchange for a riverboat casino license. Eddie Jr. never received the license and pleaded guilty to a charge of "failing to report a felony," which carried a $1 million fine and two years probation.

He was also fined by the NFL and barred from active control of the team for one year. However, more legal battles eventually led to DeBartolo giving up control of the 49ers. In 2000, his sister, Marie Denise DeBartolo York, took control of the team. Her husband, John York, played an active role with the team from 2000 to 2008, and their son, Jed York, became team president in 2009.

49ers Hall of Famers

Fred Dean (defensive end) played for San Francisco from 1981 to 1985. He was credited with 12 sacks in 11 games leading up to the team's first Super Bowl victory in 1982.

Jimmy Johnson (cornerback) played for the 49ers from 1961 to 1976. He is considered to be one of the best man-to-man defenders in NFL history.

John Henry Johnson (fullback) played for San Francisco from 1954 to 1956. He was a member of what some considered the finest backfield in NFL history, also known as "The Million Dollar Backfield" or "The Fabulous Foursome," comprising Johnson, Tittle, Perry and McElhenny.

Ronnie Lott (cornerback and safety) played for the 49ers from 1981 to 1990. He ranks fifth on the list of all-time interceptions (63) and ranks first in postseason interceptions (9). Lott played in 10 Pro Bowls and was the defensive leader of San Francisco's first four Super Bowl championship teams.

Hugh McElhenny (halfback) played for San Francisco from 1952 to 1960. He is one of only three players to gain over 11,000 yards carrying the ball.

Joe Montana (quarterback) played for San Francisco from 1979 to 1992. He retired with the highest QB rating (92.3) in history. Montana had 31 fourth-quarter comebacks, including a 92-yard game-winning drive in the final minutes of Super Bowl XXIII. He led the 49ers to four Super Bowl wins during the 1980s and was Super Bowl MVP for three of those games.

Leo "The Lion" Nomellini (defensive tackle) played every 49ers game for 14 seasons (1950–63). Nomellini played in 174 consecutive regular season games and 10 Pro Bowls. He was one of the few to be named to an all-NFL team on both offense and defense.

Joe "The Jet" Perry (fullback) played for the 49ers from 1948 to 1960 and again in 1963. He was the first player in NFL history to gain 1000 yards in two consecutive seasons, and his 9723 rushing yards made him second only to Jim Brown when he retired.

Jerry Rice (wide receiver) played for the 49ers from 1985 to 2000. He is considered by many to be the greatest wide receiver to ever play professional football. He went to 13 Pro Bowls and holds numerous all-time records for wide receivers, including receptions (1549), receiving yards (22,895) and touchdown receptions (197). Rice won three Super Bowl rings with San Francisco and caught at least one pass in 274 consecutive games from his rookie year in 1985 through September 2004.

Bob St. Clair (offensive tackle) played for the 49ers from 1953 to 1963. He once lost five teeth blocking a punt and earned all-NFL honors three times and went to the Pro Bowl five times.

Y.A. Tittle (quarterback) played for the 49ers from 1951 to 1960. He was a 17-year NFL veteran and finished his career with 33,070 passing yards and 281 touchdowns.

Bill Walsh (head coach) coached San Francisco from 1979 to 1988 and led the team to three Super Bowl titles (XVI, XIX, XXIII) over that 10-year period.

Dave "The Intimidator" Wilcox (linebacker) played for San Francisco from 1964 to 1974. He was known for effectively shutting down tight ends at the line of scrimmage and preventing them from running pass routes.

Steve Young (quarterback) played for the 49ers from 1987 to 1999. He was the most accurate passer in league history with a QB rating of 96.8. Young notched 28 300-yard passing games and holds the NFL record for most consecutive 300-yard games (six in 1998). He also led the league in passing for an NFL-record four consecutive seasons (1991–94) and his 43 rushing touchdowns rank first in pro football history by a quarterback. Young was a two-time NFL MVP (1992 and 1994), was Super Bowl XXIX MVP in 1994 and was named to the Pro Bowl for seven consecutive years (1992 to 1998).

The Legacy of Garrison Hearst

Garrison Hearst was a running back in the NFL from 1993 to 2004. His best years were with the San Francisco 49ers in 1997–98 and 2001–03. In 1997, he ran for 1019 yards and four touchdowns, becoming the 49ers' first 1000-yard rusher since Ricky Watters.

In 1998, the 49ers went 12–4, and Hearst ran for 1570 yards and seven touchdowns while averaging 5.1 yards per carry. He set a franchise record up to that point for rushing yards in a season, breaking Roger Craig's record of 1502 yards that was set in 1988. He also picked up 535 receiving yards, which gave him a combined 2105 yards on the season, another franchise record at that time. Hearst also had the longest running play in the NFL that season, running 96 yards for a game-winning touchdown in overtime against the New York Jets. The play was featured on *NFL Films* as one of the two best running plays in NFL history.

On January 19, 1999, the 49ers faced the Atlanta Falcons, and on the first play from scrimmage, Hearst incurred a horrible ankle break. However, the 49ers kept him on their roster as an inactive player even though doctors were uncertain whether he'd ever be able to play again. The team went 10–22 the next two seasons. Hearst came back in 2001 after two years of rehabilitation and became the first player in NFL history to return to football after suffering a vascular necrosis, caused by complications following surgery. He rushed for 1206 yards that season on a 4.8 average, the 49ers went 12–4 and Hearst earned the NFL Comeback Player of the Year Award.

However, in November 2002, Hearst made headlines for an entirely different reason. When a reporter from the *Fresno Bee* asked his opinion on former defensive lineman Esera Tuaolo—who had played for five different NFL teams from 1991 to 1999—coming out as gay, Hearst said, "Aww, hell no! I don't want any faggots on my team. I know this might not be what people want to hear, but that's a punk. I don't want any faggots in this locker room."

Lindsy McLean

Lindsy McLean was an athletic trainer for college and professional football teams from 1956 to 2004. He started out as a student athletic trainer at Vanderbilt University from 1956 to 1960. From 1960 to 1967, McLean worked as an assistant trainer at San Jose State University and the University of California, Santa Barbara, and he was the head athletic trainer at the University of Michigan from 1968 to 1978.

In 1979, Bill Walsh recruited him to become the head athletic trainer for the San Francisco 49ers, and McLean stayed with the team for 24 years before retiring after the 2003 season. He was inducted into the National Athletic Trainers' Association Hall of Fame in 1988.

In 2004, a feature story about Lindsy McLean appeared in *ESPN The Magazine*, in which he acknowledged that he was gay and opened up about how he was unfairly treated and harassed by some players. McLean said that many players and team officials were aware of his homosexuality when he worked for the 49ers, and he described how one player would repeatedly grab him and simulate having sex with him in front of other players and staff.

Kirk Reynolds, the 49ers' public relations director for several years, witnessed one of the incidents and was quoted in the 2004 *ESPN The Magazine* article: "There were coaches there, wives, sponsors, players, and we were all standing around waiting for the bus," he recalls. "At first, I thought the guy was joking. But it became clear it was something else. It was disturbing and bizarre."

Bill Walsh was also quoted in the article: "I'm sure bad things like that happened. There's no way I would have known these things because he was so private. If he'd come to me, he knows all hell would have broken loose. I suppose that's why he never told me." The ESPN article went on to describe a conversation McLean had with Walsh the day after McLean's retirement party in which Bill Walsh mentioned that his son, Steve Walsh, had died from AIDS in 2002.

The takeaway of the 2004 article in *ESPN The Magazine* was that there were several upstanding individuals, such as Walsh and Reynolds, who were part of the organization and supportive of McLean. However, during a time when the topic of gay players and homophobia in the NFL was getting a lot of media attention, it also made clear that Hearst's comments in 2002 were not isolated anti-gay comments but were indicative of more widespread intolerance of homosexuals in the whole NFL.

Videogate

It's obviously not advantageous for the San Francisco 49ers, of all NFL franchises, to have an anti-gay or homophobic image. However, the Hearst anti-gay comment in 2002 was not an isolated incident, and NFL players around the league were making similar statements both publicly and privately. In addition, the ESPN article definitely caused a great deal of friction for the 49ers.

So in 2004, the public relations director for the team, Kirk Reynolds—originally from Santa Barbara—launched an internal diversity training program that was meant to educate the players about how damaging insensitive comments and behavior could be to their image and to the team. The training had several goals, including teaching the players how to field questions from reporters involving sensitive subject matter.

On the surface, this may seem like a relatively straightforward mission. You simply sit everyone down and spell it out. Unfortunately, the organization had already tried that for several years—it's called "media training." And the players obviously weren't paying attention because the key messages weren't quite getting through to them.

The new approach was to put together a comprehensive training program and produce a few humorous and politically incorrect videos to get the politically *correct* points across. Again, it's important to stress that these were meant for internal use only and, taken out of context, could obviously be found offensive. It's also important to remember who the audience was: professional athletes who clearly weren't responding to more traditional forms of sensitivity training. The turn of events that followed, which cost Reynolds his job, were truly tragic.

Anyone who has ever met Kirk Reynolds will tell you that he's a true professional and is one of the most tolerant, open-minded and thoughtful individuals in the sports industry. However, when copies of the videos that the 49ers were using as part of their media training were leaked to the press in 2005, Reynolds was thrown under the team bus.

The *San Francisco Chronicle* portrayed him as a public relations director who produced "racist and sexist" videos. Reynolds was made out to be a bigot who enjoyed racially insensitive jokes, loved hanging out with topless blondes at strip clubs and was against same-sex marriage. The team lawyer for the 49ers, Ed Goines, described the production of the videos—which were intended to hopefully curb racist, sexist and otherwise insensitive comments and behavior—as being "absolutely contradictory to the ideals and values of the San Francisco 49ers."

Unfair Portrayal

The big problem here was that the way Reynolds was portrayed wasn't consistent with the rest of his career and the other eight years he worked with the 49ers' organization. Most everyone that he dealt with viewed him as someone who was willing to take a bullet for the ideals of equality and diversity. Chris

Bull wrote an article for ESPN.com in 2005 in which he summed up the situation pretty well: "This is a cautionary tale of how style and substance get confused in the media whirlwind and how a good man can be brought down in the process."

Case in point was that, in 2004, when Lindsy McLean spoke about the sexual harassment he suffered with the organization for over 20 years, Reynolds supported McLean even though he knew the revelations would be damaging. He also tried to get Hearst to talk about his admiration for McLean for helping him through his two-year rehabilitation process from 1999 to 2001. And Reynolds, who was one of Bill Walsh's closest confidantes and was the person Walsh asked to organize his memorial service before he passed away in 2007, never once attempted to extinguish the story that Bill's son had died from leukemia in 2002 instead of from AIDS, which was the true situation.

Furthermore, Kirk Reynolds was so angered by the abuse he saw McLean endure that he did what hardly any other public relations director for a professional team would ever do: he spoke up and named names. Instead of putting pressure on McLean not to name names, he took some heat away from McLean by naming the offending player himself—simply because Reynolds felt that it was important that the player be held accountable for what he did.

Positive Results

It was this history that inspired the 49ers mandatory diversity training program initiated by Reynolds in 2004, involving the infamous videos—but the truth was that the players responded to it. In fact, many of them went from hating the idea of having to sit through the education to raving about how effective the overall program had been in bringing the team closer together.

The training helped players realize that even if words like "homo," "queer" and "faggot" weren't directed toward gay individuals, they might unintentionally offend a teammate who might have a gay relative or friend. It also helped them to understand how being part of a team that was tied to such a diverse city called for more tact and thoughtfulness than they had demonstrated in the past with other teams.

Lindsy McLean helped the organization realize that they weren't promoting a healthy environment, and Kirk Reynolds successfully got through to a notoriously tough audience when it comes to sensitive issues. In fact, the diversity training program he put together was widely considered to be an effective model, but it was upstaged by the release of videotapes that should never have been watched out of context.

The videos were without a doubt unorthodox, and parts of the tapes can certainly be considered offensive and crude to someone outside the target audience. However, it's the opinion of many that Kirk Reynolds shouldn't have been fired by the 49ers for producing those videos. He was the first to publicly admit that he used "awful judgment" and apologized to everyone and anyone that was offended.

Fortunately, those who knew the "true" Kirk Reynolds never gave up on him, and he doesn't appear to have lost any credibility over the incident. In fact, after working for a few years as a public relations and communications professional for Bill Walsh, Ronnie Lott and several sports-related companies, he took a job as the vice president of public affairs for the PAC-12 Conference in 2010.

T.O.

In 1996, the San Francisco 49ers drafted Terrell Owens. In October of that first season, he scored his first touchdown—a fourth quarter, 45-yard touchdown pass from Steve Young to tie the game that the 49ers ended up winning 28–21.

In 1997, Jerry Rice tore his ACL (anterior cruciate ligament), and T.O. stepped into the spotlight. He helped the 49ers win 13 games that season and finished with 936 receiving yards. Owens was credited with eight touchdowns during the regular season and notched another touchdown in the playoffs.

T.O. had his first 1000-yard season in 1998— 67 receptions for 1097 yards and 14 touchdowns. In the wild-card playoff game, he also caught the game-winning touchdown for a 30–27 comeback victory.

In 1999, Steve Young and the 49ers were struggling, and Owens had only 60 catches for 754 yards and four touchdowns. Young retired at the end of that season, and Jeff Garcia came in as starting quarterback.

On December 17, 2000, T.O. had a record-breaking 20 receptions for 283 yards in a 17–0 San Francisco victory. And he finished the 2000 season with 1451 receiving yards and 13 touchdowns. The next season, Owens recorded 16 touchdowns and 1412 receiving yards.

In 2002, San Francisco won the NFC West title, and T.O. had 100 catches for 1300 yards and 13 touchdowns. And in the wild-card playoff game, Owens had two touchdown catches and caught two 2-point conversions in a 49ers 39–38 victory.

In 2003, San Francisco ended up with a losing record of 7–9. At this point, T.O. wanted to move on and insinuated that quarterback Jeff Garcia was gay in a *Playboy* magazine interview. As a result of his comments and his expressed desire to leave the 49ers, Owens constantly made headlines. San Francisco tried to trade Owens to the Baltimore Ravens because they asserted that his agent had missed the deadline to void the remaining years on his contract.

Meanwhile, T.O. disputed the assertion, believing that he was a free agent and he reached a contract agreement with the Philadelphia Eagles. The whole mess ended up in arbitration, and the three teams eventually reached a settlement. Owens ended up in Philadelphia for the 2004 season and reportedly landed a seven-year, $49 million contract with a $10 million signing bonus.

T.O. Celebrations While with the 49ers

January 9, 1999 (San Francisco at Atlanta): Owens caught a long touchdown pass against the Atlanta Falcons and then mimicked the Falcons' signature touchdown dance, the "dirty bird." And to make sure he really got the folks in Atlanta riled up, he made a slashing-the-throat gesture at the end of his celebration. The 49ers ended up losing the game 18–20.

September 24, 2000 (San Francisco at Dallas): T.O. celebrated his two touchdown receptions by running to midfield and dancing on the Cowboys' famous star logo. During his second celebratory dance on the star, Dallas safety George Teague tackled Owens to the ground. Teague was ejected from the game; T.O. was suspended for a week and fined $24,000. San Francisco won that game 41–24.

October 14, 2002 (San Francisco at Seattle): Owens pulled a Sharpie marker out of his sock during *Monday Night Football* in order to sign the touchdown-scoring football he'd just caught. He then gave the ball to his financial adviser, who was in the stands. T.O. wasn't fined, but the stunt did prompt the league to adopt a new rule banning players from carrying "foreign objects" with them on the field. The 49ers won the game 28–21, and Owens had six catches for 84 yards and two touchdowns.

December 15, 2002 (Green Bay at San Francisco): T.O. ran to a row of 49ers cheerleaders beyond the end zone after a touchdown, borrowed two pompoms and then did his own spontaneous celebration routine. The 49ers lost the game 14–20.

November 17, 2003 (Pittsburgh at San Francisco): Owens wore a wristband with the words "The Answer" (the widely known nickname for NBA standout Allen Iverson) on it during *Monday Night Football*. After catching a 61-yard touchdown pass, he pointed to the wristband to draw attention to it. The 49ers ended up winning the game 30–14.

December 14, 2003 (San Francisco at Cincinnati): T.O. scored a touchdown, ran to a snow pile at the edge of the field and threw snow at the fans. The 49ers ended up losing the game 38–41.

Finger

Ronald Mandel Lott, also known as "Ronnie," went to high school in Rialto, California, played college ball for the University of Southern California and was a cornerback/safety in the NFL from 1981 to 1995. He played for the San Francisco 49ers from 1981 to 1990 and is regarded as one of the hardest-hitting defensive players to ever play the game. Ronnie is also the subject of an often exaggerated, but still noteworthy, story involving his finger.

It was the final game of the 1985 regular season, and the 49ers were playing the Dallas Cowboys in San Francisco on December 22. In true Ronnie Lott style, number 42 laid a massive hit on Cowboys' running back Timmy Newsome. The collision resulted in Lott mangling his left pinky. The 49ers ended up beating Dallas 31–16.

Myth: Ronnie had the team doctor amputate his finger on the sideline during the game so that he could continue playing.

Reality: Lott had his fingers taped up so he could continue playing the game, as well as the game the following week. However, he was obviously in a great deal of pain. When the season was over, he had two choices as he prepared for the 1986 season: to undergo a complicated operation involving bone and skin grafting and the placement of pins in his hand, which meant possibly missing playing time and having to worry about re-injury, or simply to have the top of his pinky finger amputated. Ronnie chose door number two and ended up having a great season. The 49ers made another playoff appearance, and Lott went to his third Pro Bowl.

Ronnie Lott had a phenomenal career in the NFL. He earned four Super Bowl rings (XVI, XIX, XXIII, XXIV) with the 49ers and was selected for 10 Pro Bowls (1981–84 and 1986–91).

However, despite being incredibly tough and having a reputation as a vicious hitter, Ronnie Lott is a very bright guy with a big heart. In fact, after his playing days were over, he not only became a successful businessman and investor in the Silicon Valley, but he also started a great nonprofit group based in Redwood City called All Stars Helping Kids, which has a mission to "promote a safe, healthy and rigorous learning environment for disadvantaged children in low-income communities."

The following quote from Ronnie gives us a little insight into what drives him: "In our society, we're starving for people to step up and make a difference. I want to be one of those people. I don't want to walk away from my life feeling that I didn't do enough."

Oakland Raiders

Team History

The Oakland Raiders have had a colorful professional football history. It all began on January 30, 1960, when the city of Oakland was awarded the eighth

American Football League (AFL) franchise. The city managed to find several local investors and a limited partnership was created to take ownership of the team. The owners ran a "name the team" contest in the *Oakland Tribune* and the winning name was the "Oakland Señors." However, nine days later, they decided to change the name to the "Oakland Raiders," which had actually finished third in the contest.

The Raiders started off with three consecutive losing seasons—going 6–8 in 1960, 2–12 in 1961 and 1–13 in 1962—and went through three head coaches. By 1961, the team was down to two owners, Wayne Valley and Ed McGah, and were taking out loans just to stay afloat. Before entering the 1963 season, the Raiders hired 33-year-old Al Davis to be the new head coach and general manager. Davis had been an assistant coach for the Los Angeles Chargers (now the San Diego Chargers) from 1960 to 1962 and was, at the time, the youngest person in pro football history to be hired as a head coach or general manager.

In 1963, Al Davis changed the team colors to silver and black (the same colors the team wears today) and changed their offensive scheme. And in their fourth AFL season, the Raiders achieved their first winning season with a record of 10–4, and Al Davis was named the AFL's Coach of the Year. In 1964, the team went 5–7–2 and managed another winning season in 1965, with a record of 8–5–1.

In April 1966, Davis left the Raiders briefly to take a job as commissioner of the AFL. However, a couple of months into it, the AFL decided to merge with the

National Football League (NFL), so his position was dropped. In July 1966, Al Davis paid $18,000 for a 10-percent interest in the team and was put in charge of football operations.

The Madden Years

In 1967, Davis hired John Rauch to be the fifth head coach for the Oakland Raiders, and he also hired John Madden as linebacker coach that year. The staff changes proved to be positive, and the Raiders won the AFL Championship that season. They earned a trip to Super Bowl II but lost to the Green Bay Packers, who were then being coached by the great Vince Lombardi. The Raiders also had strong years in 1968 and 1969. They won the Western Division title each of those years before losing in the AFL Championship games to teams that went on to win the Super Bowl.

Rauch resigned to take the head-coaching job with the Buffalo Bills, and the 32-year-old Madden became the Raiders' sixth head coach in February 1969. As with Al Davis, John Madden was the youngest head coach in pro football history up to that point.

In 1970, the AFL and NFL merged as planned, and the Raiders became one of the Western Division teams of the American Football Conference (AFC). John Madden remained head coach of the team for 10 seasons, and the Raiders finished with winning records for all of those years. In 1977, the Oakland Raiders grabbed their first Super Bowl by beating the Minnesota Vikings 32–14, and Madden retired after the 1978 season at the age of 42. He was the youngest coach in pro football history to win 100 regular season games.

To Los Angeles and Back

In 1979, former Raiders' quarterback Tom Flores (1960–66) was promoted from assistant coach to become the new head coach of the team. Flores was born in Sanger and was the first Hispanic quarterback and head coach in pro football history. The Raiders won the Super Bowl again in 1981, and the team moved to Los Angeles in 1982. In 1984, the Los Angeles Raiders won the Super Bowl, and Tom Flores moved to the front office after the 1987 season.

Al Davis has made a lot of changes to the Raiders since their last Super Bowl win in 1984, and controversial player trades and coach firings have been the norm. He's been at the center of numerous feuds, and it's well known that he has a great deal of animosity for the NFL. Mike Shanahan was head coach for the team from 1988 to 1989, and then Art Shell took over from 1990 to 1994.

The Raiders moved back to Oakland at the end of the 1994 season, and Mike White was hired as the new head coach from 1995 to 1996 before Joe Bugel took over in 1997. Jon Gruden had the job from 1998 to 2001. Bill Callahan took over from 2002 to 2003. Norv Turner gave it a go from 2004 to 2005. Art Shell came back in 2006. Lane Kiffin got a shot at leading the team in 2007, and Tom Cable has been the head coach since 2008.

From 2003 to 2008, the Raiders had a 24–72 record. However, they are the only team other than the Pittsburgh Steelers to have played in the Super Bowl in four different decades. They have made it to the Super

Bowl five times over the years, have three Super Bowl wins and have played in their conference/league championship game in every decade since the franchise began.

In 2007, Al Davis, now in his 80s, sold a minority stake in the Raiders for $150 million and vowed to stay involved with the operation of the team until the Raiders either won two more Super Bowls or he died, whichever came first.

Raider Nation

The Oakland Raiders play in the Oakland Coliseum, and fans of the team are unofficially called the "Raider Nation." Sections 104 to 107 are known as the "Black Hole" because they are usually home to the rowdiest fans. Author Hunter S. Thompson, who was a Raider fan later in his life, once wrote, "The massive Raider Nation is beyond doubt the sleaziest and rudest and most sinister mob of thugs and wackos ever assembled." These over-the-top fans seem to inspire rowdy play on the field, and the aggressive play on the field appears to escalate the rowdiness of the fans.

The Hit

On August 12, 1978, the Oakland Raiders were playing a pre-season game against the New England Patriots at the Oakland Coliseum. Raiders' defensive back Jack Tatum, also known as "The Assassin," made a controversial hit on Patriots wide receiver Darryl Stingley. The impact compressed Stingley's spinal cord and broke his fourth and fifth vertebrae. As a result, he spent the rest of his life as a quadriplegic.

Prior to that game, Darryl Stingley, a young player at the top of his career, had negotiated a contract extension that would have made him one of the highest paid receivers in the NFL. The hit became a symbol of violence in football and received a great deal of public attention. In response to the tragic outcome, the NFL made some rule changes in order to prevent overly aggressive play. Raiders head coach at the time, John Madden, rushed to the hospital after the game and became a close friend of Stingley's.

Dirty Raiders

Besides Jack Tatum, several Oakland Raiders have been labeled over the years as overly aggressive and even "dirty," including:

Skip Thomas (cornerback): His vicious tackling earned him the nickname "Dr. Death." He played for the Raiders from 1972 to 1977.

Lyle Alzado (defensive end): Described as a violent and combative player, he played for Oakland from 1982 to 1985 and was the inspiration for the NFL rule against throwing your helmet.

Steve Wisniewski (offensive guard): He played for the Raiders from 1989 to 2001 and was once number four on an ESPN list of the dirtiest players in history of any professional sport.

Kevin Gogan (offensive guard): He played for the Raiders from 1994 to 1996 and was once named "Dirtiest Player in the NFL" by *Sports Illustrated*.

Bill Romanowski (linebacker): Also known as "Romocop," he played for Oakland from 2002 to 2003 and was forced to retire after confronting teammate

Marcus Williams after a play, ripping off his helmet and crushing Williams' eye socket with a punch.

Harrison Suspension

On October 20, 2002, at the Oakland Coliseum, the Oakland Raiders hosted the San Diego Chargers. In the first quarter, strong safety Rodney Harrison, who was widely regarded as one of the dirtiest players in the NFL when he played, put a helmet-to-helmet hit on Oakland Raiders' receiver Jerry Rice on an incomplete pass at the San Diego nine-yard line. The NFL suspended Harrison, who was playing for the Chargers at the time, without pay for one game. San Diego ended up winning the game 27–21 in overtime.

This was one of many fines and suspensions Rodney Harrison racked up during his career for illegal hits, not to mention his use of human growth hormone. However, since the hit involved Jerry Rice, who was already a legend in the NFL by then, and Harrison, who had such a poor on-field reputation, this particular illegal hit received a lot of attention.

San Diego Chargers

Bought by the Hiltons

In 1959, the Los Angeles Chargers were one of eight teams to be added to the American Football League (AFL) and originally played in Los Angeles before relocating to San Diego in 1961. The team's first owner was Barron Hilton, son of the founder of Hilton Hotels.

For those of you who don't keep up on tabloid news, Barron is also Paris Hilton's grandfather. In 2007, he axed her inheritance by $60 million following her 2003 sex tape and multiple drunk-driving offenses, stating that he didn't want to leave "unearned wealth" to his family. However, you probably won't be seeing Paris at the homeless shelter anytime soon—her estimated net worth is still around $50 million, and she reportedly "earns" between $25,000 and $100,000 to appear at parties and clubs.

Franchise History

The franchise's first head coach was Sid Gillman, who led the team from 1960 to 1971. Under his direction, the Chargers got off to a strong start, winning the AFL West Division Championship in 1960, 1961, 1963, 1964 and 1965, and the AFL Championship in 1963. In 1966, Hilton sold the Chargers to a group headed up by Eugene Klein and Sam Schulman.

In 1984, Alex Spanos purchased a majority interest in the franchise from Eugene Klein and eventually bought out the other minority-share owners until he controlled 97 percent of the team. The only other ownership partner is George Pernicano, who originally invested in the team in the 1960s. Dean Spanos, Alex's son, has been handling a lot of the daily operations since 1994, and in 2007, *Forbes* estimated the San Diego Chargers to be worth $826 million.

Since joining the National Football League in 1970, the Chargers have been to the playoffs 10 times and have made four appearances in the AFC Championship game. In 1992, San Diego became the only NFL team to start a season with four straight losses and still make the playoffs. In January 1995, to end of the 1994 season, the Chargers made it to Super Bowl XXIX but lost to the San Francisco 49ers 49–26. In 2008, the Chargers became the only team to go 4–8 for their first 12 games and still make it to the playoffs. The San Diego Chargers remain one of 14 teams in the NFL to have never won a Super Bowl.

Chargers Hall of Famers

Sid Gillman (head coach/general manager), 1960–69 and 1971; he won five division titles in the AFL's first six years.

Ron Mix (offensive lineman), 1960–69; he had only two holding penalties in 10 years.

Lance Alworth (wide receiver), 1962–70; he made catches in 96 straight games.

Dan Fouts (quarterback), 1973–87; he was the third player ever to pass for more than 40,000 yards.

Fred Dean (defensive end), 1975–81; he was named All-Pro in 1980 and 1981.

Charlie Joiner (wide receiver), 1976–86; he played 18 seasons and 239 games, the most ever for a wide receiver when he retired in 1986.

Kellen Winslow (tight end), 1979–87; he had 89 receptions in 1980 and 88 receptions in 1981 and 1983.

Freezer Bowl

The 1981 AFC Championship game between the San Diego Chargers and the Cincinnati Bengals became known as the "Freezer Bowl." Despite the Bengals dominance over the Chargers during their regular season matchup, all signs pointed to an exciting, high-energy game when the two division rivals met to decide who would move on to the Super Bowl.

The Chargers had just been through what is now known as the "Epic in Miami," where they beat the Dolphins in overtime in a game that saw temperatures soar to over 90°F, with a few extra degrees added for the intense humidity. It was an unpleasant game, but the Chargers managed to pull out of the heat with a win. Going into Cincinnati for the AFC Championship, however, the Chargers got the complete opposite of what they had just experienced.

Before even taking the field, Chargers running back, Hank Bauer, went out and tested the field conditions. "When I came out of that tunnel...man, [the wind] just hit you like somebody threw 100 knives at you." He returned to the locker room to tell his teammates about the conditions. "Whatever you got on, take it off. Number one, you won't be able to move [with all the layers], and number two, it ain't gonna help."

The temperature on the field had dropped to an incredible −59°F with the wind chill. That's cold enough to freeze exposed skin in just a matter of minutes, but despite the record-setting cold, the game went on and the players battled through the conditions. The Bengals offensive line was a little more accustomed to the freezing temperatures than the Chargers and played the entire game with bare arms.

Under those conditions, it was hard to survive, let alone play football, and the warmer climate–conditioned

Chargers ended up losing the game by a final score of 27–7.

College Football

The Big Game

There's a lot of hype every year surrounding the annual fall football game between rivals the Cal Bears (University of California, Berkeley) and the Stanford Cardinals (Stanford University in Palo Alto). This matchup has been named the "Big Game" and is without a doubt the biggest college football event in the San Francisco Bay Area. The first Big Game was held on March 19, 1892, in San Francisco and has become one of the longest rivalries in NCAA Division 1 history. Stanford leads the series with a record of 55–47–11, but Cal has won seven of the last eight Big Games following a seven-game Stanford winning streak. The venue for the Big Game alternates between the two universities each year—Berkeley in even-numbered years, and Stanford in odd-numbered years.

Herbert Hoover, U.S. president from 1929 to 1933, was the Stanford team manager for the first Big Game in 1892. The name "Big Game" was first used in 1900, and the game was played on Thanksgiving Day in San Francisco. Tragedy also struck that day when the roof of S.F. and Pacific Glass Works collapsed. Thirteen people died and 78 were injured while trying to watch the game from the top of the building.

Since 1933, the winner of the game has been awarded the "Stanford Axe" and, before the NCAA instituted overtime in 1996, if the game ended in a tie, the Axe stayed with the team that already possessed it. The Axe has been stolen several times by students from both universities, starting with the very first Big Game in 1892.

The Play

One of the wildest games between Cal and Stanford was played on November 20, 1982, in Berkeley. "The Play" refers to a last-second and very controversial kickoff return that is still regarded as one of the most memorable plays in college football history and ranks among the most memorable moment of all American sports. Stanford's quarterback for the game was John Elway, who was playing in his last regular season game before heading off to become a star NFL player—Elway has been enshrined in both the Pro Football Hall of Fame as well as the College Football Hall of Fame.

Cal was leading Stanford 19–17 late in the fourth quarter. However, Elway completed a 29-yard pass on fourth-and-17 on his own 13-yard line and then managed to get the ball within field goal range for kicker Mark Harmon. The Cardinals' coach, Paul Wiggin, told Elway to call a timeout with eight seconds left on the clock in order to leave enough time for a second field-goal attempt in the event that Stanford drew a penalty on the first try. The 35-yard kick was good, and Stanford took a 20–19 lead with four seconds left on the clock. However, the Cardinals were flagged for "excessive celebration" and a 15-yard penalty was enforced on the kickoff, so Stanford had to kick off from their 25-yard line instead of their 40.

The Laterals

With just four seconds left in the game, Fred Von Appen, Stanford's special teams coach, called for a "squib kick." A squib kick is a short, low, line-drive kickoff that is meant to bounce on the ground quite a bit before it can be picked up by a member of the receiving team. And because it is kicked short, it forces the slower blockers at the front to recover the ball instead of allowing it to get into the hands of a faster kick returner in the backfield. As a result of all of the confusion, only 10 players took the field for Cal, one player short but still legal.

Now comes the good part: Harmon squibbed the kick as instructed, and Cal defensive back Kevin Moen was the first player to pick the ball up at Cal's 45-yard line. Moen then lateraled the ball to teammate Richard Rodgers. However, Rodgers was surrounded, so he lateraled to teammate Dwight Garner. Garner gained five yards and managed to lateral the ball back to Rodgers just as he was being tackled. At this exact moment, several Stanford players on the sideline and the entire Stanford band ran onto the field in celebration, thinking that Garner had been tackled and the game was over. But, as you can imagine, this didn't stop the action on the field.

Rodgers dodged another Stanford player and was able to get to the middle of the field, where other Cal players were ready for the next lateral. Rodgers lateraled to teammate Mariet Ford at the Stanford 45. By now, all 144 members of the Stanford band were spread out over the end zone that Cal was advancing toward, and some band members were even 20 yards downfield.

Ford escaped a tackle and was sprinting into the band before being slaughtered by three Stanford players at the 27-yard line. However, before Ford went down, he threw a blind lateral over his shoulder, which was caught by Moen, who had started the whole play. Moen then charged toward the end zone, managing to dodge one Stanford player while outrunning another. Moen plowed through the Stanford band members for the winning touchdown and completed the play by spiking the ball on the head of Stanford trombone player Gary Tyrrell.

The Review

Even though the officials hadn't signaled the touchdown, the Cal players were in full-force celebration mode. Stanford argued to the officials that Dwight Garner's knee had been down before he was able to release the ball. So the officials huddled, but the chaos of the entire play and the fact that a lot of action took place in the middle of the Stanford band meant the call was a challenging one to make.

The game referee, Charles Moffett, later described that huddle in an interview:

"I called all the officials together and there were some pale faces. The penalty flags were against Stanford for coming onto the field. I say, 'Did anybody blow a whistle?' They say, 'No.' I say, 'Were all the laterals legal?' 'Yes.' Then the line judge, Gordon Riese, says to me, 'Charlie, the guy scored on that.' And I said, 'What?' I had no idea the guy had scored. Actually, when I heard that, I was kind of relieved. I thought we really would have had a problem if they hadn't scored, because, by the rules, we could have awarded a touchdown [to Cal] for [Stanford] players coming onto the field. I didn't want to have to make that call.

"I wasn't nervous at all when I stepped out to make the call; maybe I was too dumb. Gee, it seems like it was yesterday. Anyway, when I stepped out of the crowd, there was dead silence in the place. Then when I raised my arms, I thought I had started World War III. It was like an atomic bomb had gone off."

The referees determined that Cal had scored and that none of the laterals were illegal, which made the fact that the Stanford band and sideline players had rushed the field before the play was over—which normally would have resulted in an "illegal participation penalty"—irrelevant.

The final score was Cal 25, Stanford 20.

The Fallout

The Cal touchdown ruling was extremely controversial at the time, and "The Play" is still the subject of intense debates between die-hard fans of the two teams. The crux of the controversy is the legality of two of the five laterals as well as the chaos on the field. The NCAA didn't adopt instant replay until 2005, so the officials didn't have the option of consulting recorded television footage at the time. However, video replays of Garner being tackled and the exact moment that his knee touched the ground are inconclusive because of the camera angles. And the fifth lateral from Mariet Ford to Kevin Moen, which some believe to be an illegal forward pass, is also difficult to analyze.

Either way, Stanford was guilty of illegal participation, and two game officials immediately threw penalty flags against Stanford for having too many men on the field. And since a football game can't end on a defensive penalty, Cal would have at least been given the chance to run one unclocked play from scrimmage or even been awarded a touchdown for the interference.

The Heisman

Did you know? More winners of the most prestigious player award in college football—the Heisman Trophy—have come from California than from any other U.S. state. In fact, 14 Heisman winners were born and played high school football in California:

1946: **Glenn Davis**, from Bonita High School in La Verne (college: United States Military Academy at West Point)

1964: **John Huarte**, from Mater Dei High School in Santa Ana (college: University of Notre Dame)

1965: **Mike Garrett**, from Roosevelt High School in Los Angeles (college: University of Southern California)

1967: **Gary Beban**, from Sequoia High School in Redwood City (college: University of California, Los Angeles)

1968: **O.J. Simpson**, from Galileo High School in San Francisco (college: University of Southern California)

1970: **Jim Plunkett**, from William C. Overfelt High School and James Lick High School in East San Jose (college: Stanford University)

1979: **Charles White**, from San Fernando High School in San Fernando (college: University of Southern California)

1981: **Marcus Allen**, from Abraham Lincoln High School in San Diego (college: University of Southern California)

1992: **Gino Torretta**, from Pinole Valley High School in Pinole (college: University of Miami)

1994: **Rashaan Salaam**, from La Jolla Country Day School in La Jolla (college: Colorado University at Boulder)

1998: **Ricky Williams**, from Patrick Henry High School in San Diego (college: University of Texas)

2002: **Carson Palmer**, from Santa Margarita High School in Rancho Santa Margarita (college: University of Southern California)

2004: **Matt Leinart**, from Mater Dei High School in Santa Ana (college: University of Southern California)

2005*: **Reggie Bush**, from Helix High School in La Mesa (college: University of Southern California)

* The Heisman Trophy was returned by USC in 2010 because it was discovered that Bush had accepted improper benefits while at USC.

Trojans

The University of Southern California (USC) has a strong college football tradition that dates back to 1888. The team is part of the Pacific-12 Conference (PAC-12), plays at the Division 1 level and has won 11 National Collegiate Athletic Association (NCAA) national championships.

In 1888, the first USC football team was assembled by a few USC students/players, including Arthur Carroll, Frank Suffel and Henry Goddard. In 1893, they joined the Intercollegiate Football Association of Southern California, which was made up of USC, Occidental College, Throop Polytechnic Institute and Chaffey College.

In 1905, USC played their first game out of Southern California when they went up to Palo Alto, California, to play against Stanford but lost 16–0. The two teams didn't face off again until 1918, when their rivalry officially began. However, USC did play Oregon State in 1914, UC Berkeley and Oregon in 1915 and Arizona in 1916.

USC's football team was originally called the Methodists, then they were called the Wesleyans, but in 1912, they adopted the name Trojans. From 1911 to 1913, USC briefly dropped their football program and replaced it with rugby (as did Stanford and Cal) and had truly awful results. During that time, Owen R. Bird, a sportswriter for the *Los Angeles Times*, gave the team the nickname "Trojans" because he observed that they were facing off against larger and better-prepared rivals.

In 1922, the Trojans joined the Pacific Coast Conference. The head coach for the team at the time was Gus "Gloomy" Henderson, and they started to experience some strong results. From 1925 to 1940, head coach Howard Jones helped develop the Trojans into one of the few nationally dominant teams, and they won their first four national titles (1928, 1931, 1932 and 1939). During the 1940s and 1950s, however, USC was much less consistent and wasn't able to win any national championships.

Back to Winning Ways

John McKay coached the team from 1960 to 1975 and helped the Trojans win four more national championships (1962, 1967, 1972 and 1974). Two USC football players also won the Heisman Trophy during this period: Mike Garrett in 1965 and O.J. Simpson in 1968.

In 1970, USC traveled to the South to face the University of Alabama, which was coached by legendary "Bear" Bryant at the time, and USC was the first "integrated" team—meaning they fielded both black and white players—to play in the state of Alabama. After the Trojans handed the non-integrated Crimson Tide team a 42–21 defeat, in which African American players scored all USC touchdowns, Bryant was able to successfully persuade the University of Alabama to integrate the Crimson Tide as well—a huge step toward racial equality in Southern sports.

From 1976 to 1982, John Robinson became the head honcho, and USC was able to claim another national championship in 1978. In 1979, Charles White won the Heisman, and in 1981 it was awarded to Marcus Allen.

USC football went through a few coaches from 1983 to 2000 but was still recognized as one of the better programs in the nation. However, the Trojans weren't able to boast any national championships, and they were having a tough time living up to the high expectations that their supporters had for the team. In fact, from 1996 to 2001, USC had an unimpressive record of 37–35, which was their worst over any five-year period since 1961.

Trojans in the 2000s

In 2001, Pete Carroll was brought on board as head coach. The Trojans finished with a 6–6 record in his first year. However, things picked up in a big way after that. USC went 11–2 in 2002, and quarterback Carson Palmer got the Heisman that season. In 2003, the Trojans had a record of 12–1 and claimed their first national championship since 1978. In 2004, quarterback Matt Leinart was awarded the Heisman, and USC won another national championship after going undefeated (13–0) all season.

In 2005, the Trojans finished the regular season 12–0 and earned the opportunity to play Texas in the Rose Bowl for the national championship. Unfortunately, they lost a close game 41–38. USC running back, Reggie Bush, was awarded the Heisman Trophy that season, but in 2010 the trophy was returned when it was discovered that Bush had accepted improper benefits such as free rent, marketing and memorabilia deals while he was attending USC.

The Trojans posted 11–2 records in both the 2006 and 2007 seasons and went 12–1 in 2008. USC also won the Pac-10 Conference Championship for seven straight years (2002–08). In 2009, the team went 9–4, and at the end of the season, Pete Carroll took the head coaching job with the Seattle Seahawks. During Carroll's first eight years leading the Trojans, USC lost only one game by more than seven points, a 27–16 loss to Notre Dame in 2001. Lane Kiffin, former head coach for the Oakland Raiders, became the head coach for the Trojans after Pete Carroll resigned.

1967 USC vs. UCLA

The USC Trojans and the University of California Los Angeles (UCLA) Bruins have been longtime rivals. One of their most memorable matchups was on November 18, 1967, at the Los Angeles Memorial Coliseum and is regarded by most as *the* best game in the USC–UCLA rivalry. UCLA was ranked number one entering the game and USC was ranked number two. Both teams also had Heisman Trophy candidates for that season. The Bruins had quarterback Gary Beban, while the Trojans had running back O.J. Simpson (yes, the same O.J. that will forever be remembered for much more notorious reasons).

The stakes for this game were very high: it would not only decide the AAWU (now the Pac-12) Conference champion, but the winner would go on to the Rose Bowl to play for the national championship.

In the fourth quarter, the game was tied at 14–14. UCLA's quarterback, Beban, was injured with bruised ribs but managed to complete a touchdown pass to put the Bruins up 20–14. However, the extra point attempt was blocked. With around 10 minutes left in the game,

Simpson ran 64 yards for a touchdown, and USC got the extra point and a narrow 21–20 win. Beban passed for 301 yards that day, and Simpson was credited with two touchdowns and 177 rushing yards.

The Trojans went on to beat Indiana in the Rose Bowl and became the national champions of the 1967 season. Beban was awarded the Heisman Trophy that year, and Simpson won it the following season. Beban was a backup quarterback for the Washington Redskins in 1968–69 before retiring in 1970. However, O.J. went on to have a successful NFL career and was inducted to the Pro Football Hall of Fame in 1985.

The Streak

The De La Salle High Spartans have redefined domination. From 1992 to 2005, De La Salle High School in Concord won an amazing 151 straight high school football games and set the national record for a winning streak, absolutely shattering the previous record of 72 in the process. De La Salle is a private Catholic, all-boys school and has gained national recognition for its high school football domination.

Bob Ladouceur began coaching the team in 1979 when he was just 25 years old. Before he took the helm, the Spartans hadn't finished a season with a winning record. However, during his reign, the team had a stunning record of 357–24–3 and was named national champion in seven different years: 1994 (ESPN), 1999 (*National Sports News Service*), 1998, 2000, 2001, 2002 and 2003 (*USA Today*). They were also crowned California state champions in 1992, 1994 to 2003, 2007 and 2009. Several De La Salle High

Spartans have since gone on to careers in the NFL, including:

- Maurice Jones-Drew (Jaguars)
- Kevin Simon (Redskins)
- Matt Gutierrez (Chiefs)
- D.J. Williams (Broncos)
- Doug Brien (49ers)
- David Loverne (Jets)
- Derek Landri (Jaguars)
- Steve Alexakos (Broncos and Giants)
- Amani Toomer (Giants and Chiefs)
- Aaron Taylor (Packers)

More California Football

Pro Football Hall of Famers

Troy Aikman (quarterback) was born in West Covina in 1966 and played in the NFL from 1989 to 2000 for the Dallas Cowboys. He led the Cowboys to three Super Bowl wins and was the winningest starting quarterback of any decade with 90 of 94 career wins in the 1990s. Aikman had 13 regular-season and four playoff, 300-yard passing games, was named to six Pro Bowls and was inducted into the Hall of Fame in 2006.

Marcus Allen (running back) was born in San Diego in 1960 and played in the NFL from 1982 to 1997 for the Los Angeles Raiders (1982–92) and Kansas City Chiefs (1993–97). He won the Heisman Trophy in 1981 and was NFL Rookie of the Year in 1982. Allen was Super Bowl XVIII MVP and NFL MVP in 1985.

He was the first player in NFL history to rush for 10,000 or more yards and catch passes for 5000-plus yards.

Career stats: 12,243 yards rushing, 5411 yards receiving and 145 touchdowns. Allen was named to six Pro Bowls and was inducted into the Hall of Fame in 2003.

Dan Fouts (quarterback) was born in San Francisco in 1951 and played in the NFL from 1973 to 1987 for the San Diego Chargers. He was the third player ever to pass for more than 40,000 yards.

Career stats: 43,040 yards, 254 touchdowns passing, 476 yards and 13 touchdowns rushing. Fouts was the NFL MVP in 1982, was named to six Pro Bowls and was inducted into the Hall of Fame in 1993.

Frank Gifford (halfback, flanker) was born in Santa Monica in 1930 and played in the NFL from 1952 to 1960 and 1962 to 1964 for the New York Giants. He played defensive back, halfback and flanker.

Career stats: 9862 combined yards, 3609 yards rushing, 367 receptions and 484 points. Gifford was NFL Player of Year in 1956, was named to seven Pro Bowls and was inducted into the Hall of Fame in 1977.

Hugh McElhenny (halfback) was born in Los Angeles in 1928 and played in the NFL from 1952 to 1964 for the San Francisco 49ers (1952–60), Minnesota Vikings (1961–62), New York Giants (1963) and Detroit Lions (1964). He scored a 40-yard touchdown on his first professional play and won All-NFL and Rookie of Year honors.

Career stats: 11,375 combined net yards over 13 years, 5281 yards rushing, 264 pass receptions and 360 points. McElhenny played in six Pro Bowls, was the

MVP of the 1958 Pro Bowl and was inducted into the Hall of Fame in 1970.

Mel Hein (offensive lineman) was born in Redding in 1909 and played for the New York Giants from 1931 to 1945. He was a 60-minute regular for 15 years and was injured once but never missed a game. He was named All-NFL for eight straight years (1933–40) and was the NFL's MVP in 1938. Hein was the first player and only offensive lineman to be named MVP, and he was inducted into the Hall of Fame in 1963.

James Lofton (wide receiver) was born in Fort Ord in 1956 and played in the NFL from 1978 to 1993 for the Green Bay Packers (1978–86), Los Angeles Raiders (1987–88), Buffalo Bills (1989–92), Los Angeles Rams (1993) and the Philadelphia Eagles (1993). He was a wide receiver and had more than 50 receptions in a season nine times. Lofton was the first NFL player to score a touchdown in the '70s, '80s and '90s. In his 16 seasons in the NFL, he caught 764 passes for 14,004 yards, which was an NFL record when he retired. Lofton played in eight Pro Bowls and was inducted into the Hall of Fame in 2003.

Ron Mix (offensive tackle) was born in Los Angeles in 1938 and played in the NFL from 1960 to 1971 for the Los Angeles/San Diego Chargers (1960–69) and the Oakland Raiders (1971). He was an offensive tackle, had only two holding penalties in 10 years and was inducted into the Hall of Fame in 1979.

Warren Moon (quarterback) was born in Los Angeles in 1956 and played in the NFL from 1984 to 2000 for the Houston Oilers (1984–93), Minnesota

Vikings (1994–96), Seattle Seahawks (1997–98) and Kansas City Chiefs (1999–2000).

Career stats: completed 3988 of 6823 passes for 49,325 yards, 291 touchdowns and 233 interceptions over 17 seasons. Moon had nine 3000-yard passing seasons, ranked third in league history and had four 4000-yard passing seasons. He was named to nine Pro Bowls and was inducted into the Hall of Fame in 2006.

Anthony Munoz (tackle) was born in Ontario in 1958 and played in the NFL from 1980 to 1992 for the Cincinnati Bengals. He was All-Pro for 11 consecutive years (1981–91) and was elected to 11 straight Pro Bowls. Munoz caught seven passes and scored four touchdowns. He was NFL Offensive Lineman of the Year in 1981, 1987 and 1988 and started at tackle in Super Bowls XVI and XXIII. Munoz was inducted into the Hall of Fame in 1998.

Pete Rozelle (commissioner) was born in South Gate in 1926 and was NFL commissioner from 1960 to 1989. He negotiated the first league-wide TV contract in 1962, managed the AFL–NFL merger and league restructuring and developed the Super Bowl into a premier event. Rozelle was inducted into the Hall of Fame in 1985.

Tex Schramm (general manager) was born in San Gabriel in 1920 and was a general manager for the Los Angeles Rams in 1956 and the Dallas Cowboys from 1960 to 1989. While at Dallas, the Cowboys had 20 straight winning seasons (1966–85). Schramm was the NFL competition committee chairman from 1966 to 1988 and was a major advocate of instant replay, special field markings and offense-enhancing rule changes. He was inducted into the Hall of Fame in 1991.

O.J. Simpson (running back) was born in San Francisco in 1947 and played in the NFL from 1969 to 1979 for the Buffalo Bills (1969–77) and the San Francisco 49ers (1978–79). He won the Heisman Trophy in 1968 and won four NFL rushing titles.

Career highlights: 2003 yards rushing in 1973 and topped 1000 yards rushing per season from 1972 to 1976.

Career stats: 11,236 yards rushing, 203 receptions, 990 yards kickoff returns and 14,368 combined net yards. Simpson was named to five Pro Bowls, was the 1973 Pro Bowl Player of the Game and was inducted into the Hall of Fame in 1985.

Bob St. Clair (tackle) was born in San Francisco in 1931 and played in the NFL for the San Francisco 49ers from 1953 to 1963. He blocked 10 field goals in 1956, was All-NFL for four years and was named to five Pro Bowls. St. Clair was inducted into the Hall of Fame in 1990.

Bill Walsh (head coach) was born in Los Angeles in 1931 and was head coach for the San Francisco 49ers from 1979 to 1988. He led the 49ers to three Super Bowl wins (XVI, XIX, XXIII) over a 10-year period, was NFL Coach of the Year in 1981 and NFC Coach of the Year in 1984. Walsh was inducted into the Hall of Fame in 1993.

Gary Zimmerman (tackle) was born in Fullerton in 1961 and played in the NFL from 1986 to 1997 for the Minnesota Vikings (1986–92) and the Denver Broncos (1993–97). He started in 169 consecutive games, and in 1991 helped the Vikings lead the NFC in rushing. Zimmerman also helped the Broncos lead the AFC in total combined yards in 1995 and the NFL in 1996 and 1997. He was named to two NFL All-Decade Teams (the 1980s and 1990s), was named to seven Pro Bowls and was inducted into the Hall of Fame in 2008.

Chapter Two

Hardball Cali-Style

Oakland Athletics
Franchise History

In 1860, James N. Kerns started the Athletic Base Ball Club in Philadelphia, and the large "A" on the uniform dates from this era. In 1866, the National Association of Base Ball Players investigated the team for paying at least three of its players. If true, the club may have been the first professional team in baseball, at least three years ahead of the Cincinnati Red Stockings.

The team officially went professional in the late 1860s and helped establish the National Association of Professional Base Ball Players (also known simply as the National Association, or NA), the first professional league for the sport that began in 1871. The Athletics were one of the most successful National Association teams and won the first pennant with a record of 21–7. The Athletics franchise eventually moved to Kansas City in 1955 before planting roots in Oakland, California, in 1968.

The Athletics franchise has won a total of nine World Series titles and four since making the move to Oakland (1972, 1973, 1974 and 1989). They've also brought home a total of 15 American League pennants, six while in Oakland (1972, 1973, 1974, 1988, 1989 and 1990).

Take Me Out of the Ball Game

All baseball players dream of making it to the World Series and, if lucky, being one of the stars responsible for helping the team win the championship. Countless players in the majors will relate stories about when they were kids, dreaming about cracking that winning home run or throwing the perfect game to win the World Series. But the reality of sport is that not everyone gets to play the hero—sometimes your team even makes it all the way to the World Series, but you don't get to play. The latter is just what happened in 1973 to Oakland Athletics second baseman Mike Andrews during the World Series against the New York Mets.

The Oakland A's had a lot of expectations heaped onto their shoulders at the start of the series, having won the championship the previous year. However, the Mets were by no means an easy pushover, ensuring that the fans would get their money's worth in entertainment. Oakland opened up the series with a tight 2–1 victory in Game 1, but things got a little more dramatic in Game 2.

Whereas the pitchers dominated Game 1, it was the players' bats that came alive in Game 2. Although Oakland took the early lead in the first inning, the

Mets pulled ahead and, by the bottom of the ninth, had a 6–4 lead on the defending champs. Undaunted, the A's managed two runs in the ninth to tie it and send the game into extra innings.

12th Inning Andrews

It was in the top of the 12th inning when things started to go wrong for one player in particular. The Mets managed to score one earned run off an RBI single by the legend Willie Mays in what turned out to be the final hit of his long illustrious career. Despite the Mets pulling ahead by one, if the A's could contain them and get through the inning, they still had a chance to win the game. But A's pitcher Rollie Fingers (yup, his real name) allowed the Mets to load up the bases, putting pressure on the A's infield to execute a perfect double play as the Mets already had one out.

The Mets' next batter was John Milner, who grounded the ball to second baseman Mike Andrews. It was a routine play that had been done a million times in practice and during games, but this time, something went wrong and the ball snuck between his legs, rolling into the outfield. The error allowed two more runs to score to make the lead 9–6.

Andrews barely had time to recover from his gaff when the very next batter hit another easy ground ball in his direction. Andrews managed to snag the ball but ended up throwing it over the first baseman's head, allowing another run to score to make it 10–6. Mercifully, the A's managed to make it out of the inning without any further damage, but Andrews' errors cost his team dearly and they needed a miracle to make the comeback. Unfortunately, the miracle did not happen and, despite the A's scoring one run to narrow the score to 10–7, the Mets won the game and tied the series.

Physically Unfit

As upset as Andrews was with himself for the unforced errors, Oakland A's owner Charles Finley was furious with his second baseman. So much so that he ordered the team's physician, Dr. Harry Walker, to declare Andrews "physically unfit" to play the remainder of the World Series due to a chronic shoulder disability. It was Finley's intention to replace the struggling Andrews with infielder Manny Trillo, but the only problem was that Andrews was perfectly healthy.

The only way to get the league to approve the sudden change in lineup would be to add Andrews' signature to the letter, but he wasn't likely to sign anything that would take him out of the World Series. Somehow, Finley managed to coerce Andrews into signing the letter, but Andrews later expressed regret at having done so, saying that Finley had threatened to destroy his baseball career if he didn't sign.

There was an immediate uproar among Andrews' teammates at Finley's underhanded techniques. Several other players threatened to pull themselves out of the remainder of the series. Others wore Andrews' jersey number on their sleeves to show their support. All the controversy was for naught, however, because once the commissioner of baseball, Bowie Kuhn, heard of Finley's underhanded tactics, he commented that the Athletics owner's actions "had the unfortunate effect of embarrassing a player who has given so many years of able service to professional baseball."

After sitting out one game because of the fallout, Andrews returned to the lineup for Game 4 at the Mets' Shea Stadium. Coming to the plate late in the game to pinch-hit, Mets fans gave Andrews a sarcastic standing ovation. After grounding out, fans once again applauded the second baseman—more for having to deal with an unscrupulous owner rather than for his hitting ability.

All the commotion and political intrigue was quickly forgotten when the A's went on to win the series in Game 7. Despite being reinserted into the lineup and helping the A's (sort of) win the World Series, Andrews was not welcomed back into the majors. His ground out in Game 4 of the series was his last major league at bat.

Fast Fact

The Mets–A's series of 1973 was the last World Series in which each team sold separate programs for their home games. Starting in 1974, Major League Baseball printed the official World Series program that was sold in both stadiums.

1989 "Quake" Series

The 1989 series was the first time the two San Francisco Bay Area Major League Baseball teams—the Oakland Athletics and the San Francisco Giants—met in a World Series. The first two games were played at the Oakland Coliseum with the A's going 2–0. Games 3 and 4 were played at Candlestick Park in San Francisco.

However, there was an unplanned interruption in the series when, on October 17 at 5:04 PM, shortly before the first pitch was to be thrown in Game 3, a major earthquake rocked the Bay Area. The Loma Prieta earthquake, with an epicenter in Santa Cruz County, caused significant damage, thousands of injuries and left 63 people dead. The World Series coverage made it the first quake in the United States in which the initial jolt was broadcast on live television.

In addition, experts credited the 1989 World Series with preventing a more massive loss of life as throngs of Bay Area viewers weren't driving on a double-decker freeway and bridge that collapsed during what would have normally been rush-hour traffic. Game 3 finally resumed 10 days later on October 27, and Oakland swept the series 4–0.

Dave "Smoke" Stewart

The MVP of the 1989 World Series, Dave "Smoke" Stewart, was the winning pitcher for the Oakland Athletics in Games 1 and 3. Stewart was born and raised in Oakland and is among a small group of African American MLB pitchers to ever win 20 or more games in a single season (he is also featured in a book entitled *The Black Aces*). Dave Stewart made his major league debut in 1978 and had an impressive career before retiring in 1995. He won 20 or more games each season for four consecutive seasons (1987–90), pitched a no-hitter on June 29, 1990, and had a 9–1 record pitching against Roger Clemens.

Hall of Fame Players for the Oakland Athletics

Famous managers such as Billy Martin and Tony LaRussa and numerous legendary players have been part of the Oakland Athletics franchise at one point or another since 1968:

Catfish Hunter (pitcher), 1965–67 (Kansas City) and 1968–74 (Oakland); he won 224 games and five World Series rings.

Reggie Jackson (right fielder), 1967 (Kansas City) and 1968–75 and 1987 (Oakland); he had 563 career home runs.

Rollie Fingers (pitcher), 1968–76; he had 341 career saves.

Rickey Henderson (left fielder), 1979–84, 1989–93, 1994–95 and 1998; he holds the all-time record for stolen bases with 1406.

Dennis Eckersley (pitcher), 1987–95; he is the only pitcher with 100 saves and 100 complete games.

Los Angeles Dodgers

Moving West

In 1956, officials from Los Angeles were looking to relocate a baseball team to their city. Their first choice was the Washington Senators, but the team ended up moving to Bloomington, Minnesota, and became the Minnesota Twins in 1961.

When Walter O'Malley, the controlling owner of the Brooklyn Dodgers from 1950 to 1979, heard that Los Angeles officials were interested in attracting a club out west, he contacted them. Before long, Los Angeles offered him a chance to buy land to build a brand-new ballpark, an opportunity he didn't have in New York. O'Malley then convinced the New York Giants, Brooklyn's rival, to move out west as well, and both teams promptly moved to California prior to the 1958 season to continue their rivalry on the West Coast.

The Los Angeles Dodgers played in the Los Angeles Memorial Coliseum from 1958 to 1961, and construction on Dodger Stadium was finished in time for the team to start playing there in 1962. The Dodgers have won five World Series titles since moving to Los Angeles (1959, 1963, 1965, 1981 and 1988) and nine National League pennants (1959, 1963, 1965, 1966, 1974, 1977, 1978, 1981 and 1988).

Bad Day at Work

The 1977 World Series pitted the returning champion New York Yankees against the Los Angeles Dodgers. The Yankees had a good team with plenty of playoff experience, but the Dodgers were by no means easy opponents. That season, the Dodgers had the first foursome of players in major league history to hit 30 or more home runs (Steve Garvey, 33; Reggie Smith, 32; Ron Cey, 30; and Dusty Baker, 30), and they had a pitching staff that led the National League in ERA, featuring pitchers Tommy John and Charlie Hough.

While the Yankees needed every game of the best-of-five American League Championship Series against the Kansas City Royals, the Dodgers easily handled the Philadelphia Phillies in four games to move on to the World Series. Both teams had finished at the top of their divisions, and the World Series promised to be a memorable one for fans.

However, from the outset of the series, the Yankee bats seemed to be having an easier time against the Dodgers pitchers, and the New York squad, managed by Billy Martin, took a commanding 3–1 series lead after four games. Although the Dodgers' bats sprang to life in Game 5 with a convincing 10–4 win over the Yanks, the Dodgers still had the monumental task of coming from behind to win the title.

Reggie

Game 6 was do-or-die for the Dodgers in front of the New York faithful that had packed into Yankee Stadium in the hopes of witnessing history. And unfortunately for Dodgers fans, history is just what the Yankees made that evening. After the Dodgers took a quick 2–0 lead in the first inning, the Yankees quickly responded with two runs of their own off a Chris Chambliss two-run homer. The Dodgers' Reggie Smith quickly put his team back up on the board with a solo shot over the fence, but the Yankees had a Reggie of their own.

Reggie Jackson stepped up to the plate in the bottom of the fourth and belted a two-run homer off the first pitch thrown by starting Dodgers pitcher Burt Hooton to give the Yankees the lead. Once they took the lead, the Yankees never looked back.

Hoping to change their luck, Dodgers manager Tommy Lasorda called the bullpen and put Elias Sosa on the mound. But Sosa's luck was no better than Hooton's, and after allowing one man on base, he gave up another homerun to Reggie Jackson on the first pitch.

With the score now 7–3, the Dodgers needed a miracle to come through alive, and Lasorda hoped that by throwing in ace pitcher Charlie Hough, he could stem some of the bleeding. It worked up until the eighth inning, when Mr. October, Reggie Jackson, walked into the batters' box to chants of "REG-GIE, REG-GIE, REG-GIE!" and again proceeded to nail the first pitch 475 feet over the fence for his third consecutive home run.

"Oh, what a blow! What a way to top it off. Forget about who the Most Valuable Player is in the World Series! How this man has responded to pressure! Oh, what a beam on his face. How can you blame him? He's answered the whole world! After all the furor, after all the hassling, it comes down to this!" said television announcer Howard Cosell after Reggie Jackson's third home run of Game 6.

Any hopes of winning Game 6 for the Dodgers left the park with that third and final Reggie Jackson home run as the Yanks finished off the series with an 8–4 win.

'77 World Series Fast Facts

Yankee manager Billy Martin and Dodger manager Tommy Lasorda were no strangers before the start of the '77 World Series. The two baseball elders had actually been in a fistfight years earlier when they were both players.

During Game 2 of the series at Yankee Stadium, a nearby abandoned school caught fire, prompting Howard Cosell to utter the famous words, "Ladies and gentlemen...the Bronx is burning."

What the Heck is a Dodger?

Los Angeles baseball fans might be disappointed to know that the name of their beloved Dodgers has nothing to do with its West Coast home and everything to do with the franchise's original home in Brooklyn, New York.

In 1884, a new franchise was added to the American Association that would be located in the densely populated area of Brooklyn, New York. When naming the team club, president Charles Byrne knew that Brooklyn was famous for the sheer number of trolleys that paraded up and down the streets. In order to get into the stadium, players and fans literally had to "dodge trolleys," and thus the team was called the Brooklyn Trolley Dodgers.

A few years later, the team became known as the Brooklyn Bridegrooms after several of the players were married during the off-season. That team eventually folded operations in 1889 and moved to the National League. The Brooklyn team continued to operate under the name Bridegrooms for several years, and then they were renamed the Superbas, a name derived from a popular vaudeville act of the time. After that, they were called the Brooklyn Robins, the Wonders, the Grays and then the Fillies.

Despite all the different names, however, none of them was used in any official capacity. Technically, the team's legal name was the Brooklyn Base Ball Club. The team did not officially become the Dodgers until 1932, when the name first appeared on the team's jerseys.

Kurt Gibson Homer as Called by Jack Buck

"But, we have a big 3–2 pitch coming here from Eckersley. Gibson swings, and a fly ball to deep right field! This is gonna be a home run! Unbelievable! A home run for Gibson! And the Dodgers have won the game, 5–4! I don't believe what I just saw! I don't believe what I just saw! Is this really happening, Bill? One of the most remarkable finishes to any World Series game...a one-handed home run by Kirk Gibson! And the Dodgers have won it...5–4! And I'm stunned, Bill. I have seen a lot of dramatic finishes in a lot of sports, but this one might top almost every other one."

Dodgers' Notables

The Los Angeles Dodgers has been the primary club for several great players and managers, including six Hall of Famers:

Walter O'Malley (owner), 1950–57 (Brooklyn) and 1958–79 (Los Angeles)

Walter Alston (manager), 1954–57 (Brooklyn) and 1958–76 (Los Angeles)

Don Drysdale (pitcher), 1956–57 (Brooklyn) and 1958–69 (Los Angeles)

Sandy Koufax (pitcher), 1955–57 (Brooklyn) and 1958–66 (Los Angeles)

Don Sutton (pitcher), 1966–80 and 1988

Tommy Lasorda (manager), 1976–96

And numerous other Hall of Famers have spent some time in the City of Angels over the years as well:

Jim Bunning (pitcher), 1969

Hoyt Wilhelm (pitcher), 1971–72

Frank Robinson (right fielder), 1972
Juan Marichal (pitcher), 1975
Eddie Murray (first baseman), 1989–91 and 1997
Gary Carter (catcher), 1991
Rickey Henderson (left fielder), 2003

Los Angeles Angels
Different Name, Same Great Place

The Angels franchise was part of the MLB expansion in 1961, and the team was originally called the Los Angeles Angels. In 1965, the club was renamed the California Angels. In 1997, the Walt Disney Company took control of the team and renamed it the Anaheim Angels. And in 2005, the club changed its name again to the Los Angeles Angels of Anaheim for marketing reasons.

In 2002, the Angels won their one and only American League pennant and went on to win the World Series that year as well.

The Many Loves of Bo Belinsky

Women love the bad boys, and Bo Belinsky had earned that reputation long before entering the majors. Raised mostly in Trenton, New Jersey, he became streetwise at an early age and was known to hustle a few innocents down at the local pool halls. It was a reputation that was well deserved and one he would carry with him throughout his career.

Picked up in the 1962 minor league draft by the Los Angeles Angels, Belinsky began his career with a series of victories that brought him instant fame. He won his first three games, and in the fourth, he made the media come running for interviews after completing a no-hitter—the first in Angels history—against the Baltimore Orioles.

Southern California sportswriters loved Belinsky because of his no-nonsense wit and unapologetic attitude that made for great newspaper copy. As good as all the attention was for Belinsky's ego, though, it literally sank his career. After the no-hitter, he went on to lose more games than he won and finished the season with a 10–11 record.

But his baseball play wasn't what garnered him the most press throughout his career—it was his extracurricular liaisons with some of the most beautiful women in the world that will ensure his name lives on in the annals of both sports and pop-culture history.

"Within days of his no-hitter, Belinsky would be heralded as sport's most original and engaging playboy-athlete," pitcher-turned-journalist Pat Jordan wrote in a 1971 *Sports Illustrated* profile. "His name would become synonymous with a lifestyle that was cool and slick and dazzling...But in time, the name Belinsky would become synonymous with something else. It would become synonymous with dissipated talent."

During Belinsky's career, it sure seemed like it was the women he was really after. While he played for the Angels, their publicity director, Irv Kaze, best summed up why Belinsky was so irresistible to women: "He's a handsome son of a bitch. You can almost feel the animal sex in him."

Among the more famous of Belinsky's female conquests were the Shah of Iran's ex-wife Queen Soroya, dancer and actress Juliet Prowse, actress Ann Margaret, Tina Louise, Connie Stevens and the tabloid sensation, blond bombshell Mamie Van Doren.

Some women even desired him so much that they went to incredible lengths just to be with him. The most extreme example happened when Belinsky returned to his hotel room late one night and was surprised to find a young admirer hanging on for dear life on the windowsill outside his room. "I had no choice but to let her in," Belinsky later recounted of the incident.

If he had focused more on baseball and less on women, he might have had a longer career. His career lasted only eight short years, and he finished with a record of 28 wins, 51 losses and an ERA of 4.10. But to Belinsky, it was a fun way to relax and, as he observed, "No one ever died of it." Maybe it was best he had a short career.

Fast Fact

Belinsky was also on the losing end of the first no-hitter ever thrown against the Angels, when in June 1962—the same year Belinsky threw the first no-hitter in Angels history—the Boston Red Sox Earl Wilson pitched to a 2–0 no-hit win over Belinsky's Angels.

Triumph of Jim Abbott

Jim Abbott is probably the best-known professional baseball player to make it to the major leagues with a significant disability. Born without a right hand, Jim Abbott was always told growing up that he could accomplish whatever he set his mind to, and just like any other regular American kid, he wanted to play baseball. He spent hours outside his home bouncing a tennis ball off the wall to exercise his reflexes and work on his throwing.

Out on the baseball field, Abbott could technically only play one position and that was pitcher. All other positions required a player to use both hands to remain effective. This is also the case for the pitcher, but Abbott figured out a unique method to achieve success on the mound.

Wearing his fielding glove on the end of his right arm while he pitched with his left hand, Abbott would quickly transfer his glove to his left hand on his follow through so that he could handle any balls that were hit back in his direction. He showed early promise on the baseball field but was equally adept as his high school's starting quarterback, leading them to the semifinals of the Michigan state championship. But baseball was Abbott's true passion, and he displayed enough potential to be drafted by the Toronto Blue Jays shortly after graduation.

Despite the offer of a big-league career on the immediate horizon, Abbott chose to pursue his education with the University of Michigan and received a full baseball scholarship. In his freshman and junior years with the Wolverines, Abbott led them to Big Ten titles and was named the most outstanding college baseball player in the United States. He ended his college career with a record of 26 wins and only eight losses and attracted the attention of the California Angels.

Without ever playing a single game in the minor leagues, Jim Abbott made his major league appearance as the Angels starting pitcher in 1989. Many had considered the move to start a pitcher with such an obvious disability as a publicity move by the struggling Angels organization, but Abbott soon proved all doubters wrong.

In his rookie season, he won 12 games and lost 12 with an ERA of 3.92. He finished fifth in voting for the Rookie of the Year award. What made Abbott different from a pitcher like "One Arm" Daily was that Abbott still had most of his arm. He was only missing his right hand because of a birth defect. Although many people doubted that he could be a significant pitcher in the majors, Abbott silenced everyone when he pitched a no-hitter on September 4, 1993, while throwing for the Yankees against the Cleveland Indians. He later rejoined the Angels organization for the 1995 and 1996 seasons.

Although he did not have the greatest statistics and most likely will not end up in the Hall of Fame, Jim Abbott's time in the big leagues was a testament of human character over adversity.

> *There are millions of people out there ignoring disabilities and accomplishing incredible feats. I've learned you can learn to do things differently, but do them just as well. I've learned that it's not the disability that defines you, it's how you deal with*

the challenges the disability presents you with. And I've learned that we have an obligation to the abilities we DO have, not the disability.

–Jim Abbott

Fast Fact

Playing his entire career within the American League, where a designated hitter takes the pitcher's place at bat, Jim Abbott never had to hit a ball in his career. However, his former teammate with the New York Yankees, Mariano Rivera, claimed to have witnessed Abbott hit several home runs during batting practice.

Notable Angels

Several great players have spent some time with the Angels over the years, and numerous other Hall of Famers have been part of the franchise at some point as well:

- **Hoyt Wilhelm** (pitcher), 1969
- **Nolan Ryan** (pitcher), 1972–79
- **Frank Robinson** (right fielder), 1973–74
- **Dick Williams** (manager), 1974–76
- **Rod Carew** (first baseman), 1979–85
- **Reggie Jackson** (right fielder), 1982–86
- **Don Sutton** (pitcher), 1985–87
- **Dave Winfield** (right fielder), 1990–91
- **Rickey Henderson** (left fielder), 1997
- **Eddie Murray** (first baseman), 1997

San Francisco Giants

From East to West

The New York Giants won 17 pennants and five World Championships (1905, 1921, 1922, 1933 and 1954) in the Big Apple, but attendance began to fall off after the 1954 season, and they thought about relocating the franchise. At first, Horace Stoneham, the majority owner of the Giants, and the other owners were leaning toward Minneapolis–St. Paul. However, George Christopher, the mayor of San Francisco, approached Stoneham to consider his city.

Around the same time, Walter O'Malley, the controlling owner of the Dodgers, was also considering moving his team to Los Angeles, but the league told him he would need a second major league team to move to the Golden State before they would permit the Dodgers to make the switch. So O'Malley convinced Stoneham to choose San Francisco, and in 1957, both the New York Giants and the Brooklyn Dodgers decided to pack their bags for California.

The San Francisco Giants played in Seals Stadium for their first two seasons. In 1960, the team moved to Candlestick Park, a stadium built on a point that overlooks San Francisco Bay. The Giants hadn't won a World Championship since 1954 and won their first one since making the move to San Francisco in 2010. This was the third longest championship drought in Major League Baseball. However, the Giants have won four National League pennants since moving to California (1962, 1989, 2002 and 2010).

BALCO and Bonds

BALCO (the Bay Area Laboratory Co-operative), was founded by Victor Conte. Officially, the company was a service business for blood and urine analysis and a manufacturer of food supplements. But slowly, Conte began making connections in the sporting world, and soon his company was connected with football stars like Bill Romanowski, sprinter Marion Jones and a handful of players in Major League Baseball. Behind closed doors, scientists at BALCO had created a then-undetectable steroid called tetrahydrogestrinone (THG) and began supplying it in 1988 to their list of high-profile athletes.

The drug was a major leap forward in steroids chemistry, far surpassing the potency of all other steroids on the illegal markets by a factor of at least 10 times. The bonus that brought so many clients to the doors of BALCO was that THG was undetectable by drug testing of the time.

Nicknamed "The Clear" because it was as clear as water, the designer drug was also a favorite because it didn't involve injections. Users were simply required to place a few droplets underneath the tongue, and results would begin to manifest rapidly. The cause of the drug's downfall was that it became so popular among professional athletes and amateurs hoping to make a mark in the Olympics. Information leaked out, and in 2002, the Federal government began an investigation of BALCO and its associates.

The investigation reached its peak when, in the summer of 2003, the U.S. Anti-Doping Agency

(USADA) received an anonymous tip and a used syringe containing the "secret" substance known as THG. With the syringe of THG, scientists were able to create a reliable testing method for the drug, and once that was established, USADA could set its sights on taking down BALCO. It wasn't long after that the U.S Anti-Doping Agency, with the support of federal authorities, raided BALCO head offices, and the list of their clients was released to the media.

Denials

Within a few short weeks, Barry Bonds and other Major League Baseball players were dragged before a grand jury to answer to the allegations of drug abuse. The moment the allegations were released to the public, Bonds categorically denied ever using steroids to enhance his physique. He claimed that the obvious growth of his body over the years was because of a strict regimen of bodybuilding, diet and legal supplements.

When it came time for Bonds to appear before the jury, he stated under oath that he had used a clear substance and a topical cream given to him by his personal trainer, Greg Anderson; Bonds claimed that Anderson had told him it was flaxseed oil and a rubbing balm for pain. Later, Bonds underwent a random drug-screening test required under baseball's new collective bargaining agreement.

"I'm glad this is finally happening," said Bonds in response to the wave of criticism he was under in the media. "They'll get the results and it will clear my name. It'll show that there's nothing behind what I've been doing [on the field] all year."

Even though Bonds passed the test, allegations continued to dog the Giants slugger as players like Gary Sheffield and Jason Giambi came forward and admitted to receiving "substances" from Barry Bonds' trainer, Greg Anderson. Then it was discovered by reporters from the *San Francisco Chronicle* that, according to leaked grand jury reports, Bonds had claimed to have "unknowingly" used steroids known as "the cream" and "the clear." There had been other allegations of Bonds using other steroids prior to 2000, but he continued to deny ever using any performance-enhancing drugs despite a handful of former teammates coming forward to admit their abuse of the illegal steroids.

With all the accusations, prosecutors dug deeper into the possibility that Bonds had lied under oath, and in 2007, he was indicted for perjury and obstruction of justice. His trial was to have started in March 2009, but late appeals have postponed the trial indefinitely. The worst-case scenario for Bonds is that if he is ever brought up on those charges and found guilty, he would face significant jail time. At the time of this writing, there has been no further movement in the case against Bonds.

Despite the denials, Barry Bonds' name in the history of baseball has been permanently linked with the BALCO affair, therefore tainting his remarkable achievements. No matter what side you fall on in the case, it is impossible not to wonder about Bonds' involvement and use of drugs, given his incredible transformation from slender athlete to monster home-run slugger. As the history of his career is written, the asterisk beside his 762 career home runs will always haunt Barry Bonds' legacy.

Giants' Curse

Like the Boston Red Sox's "Curse of the Bambino" and the Chicago Cubs' "Curse of the Billy Goat," the San Francisco Giants have a curse of their own.

The Giants' curse began at the end of the 1957 season, when it was first announced that the franchise was moving to sunny San Francisco. New York Giants fans were so upset over the move that they gathered at the Giants' home park, the Polo Grounds (located in New York's Coogan's Bluff), and publicly professed that the Giants would never win a World Series while the team was located in California.

For decades, the words spoken at Coogan's Bluff cursed the Giants against winning the championship, but in 2010, the team finally tossed off the shackles from the past by beating the Texas Rangers in five games to win the World Series. The city of San Francisco can now boast that it is the home of a World Series Champion and, with the curse behind them, maybe another victory is in the cards for the Giants.

Hall of Famers

The San Francisco Giants have five players in the Hall of Fame:

Willie Mays (center fielder), 1951–57 (New York) and 1958–72 (San Francisco)

Orlando Cepeda (first baseman), 1958–66

Willie McCovey (first baseman), 1959–73 and 1977–80

Juan Marichal (pitcher), 1960–73
Gaylord Perry (pitcher), 1962–71

In addition, several other Hall of Fame players have spent a little time in the city by the bay:

Duke Snider (center fielder), 1964
Warren Spahn (pitcher), 1965
Joe Morgan (second baseman), 1981–82
Steve Carlton (pitcher), 1986
Rich Gossage (pitcher), 1989
Gary Carter (catcher), 1990

San Diego Padres

Franchise History

The San Diego Padres began as a minor league team in the Pacific Coast League from 1936 to 1968. Since San Diego is rich in Spanish mission history, the name "Padre" was adopted by the team as a show of respect for the European missionaries that descended on the area from Spain. In 1769, Father Juniper Serra founded the first mission in California, which was also the first European settlement in the state.

The San Diego Padres became a Major League Baseball team in 1969. They have won two National League pennants (1984 and 1998) and five West Division titles (1984, 1996, 1998, 2005 and 2006), but have yet to bring home a World Series win.

Win or Move

It is a sad thing to admit, but the history of the San Diego Padres is not one rich in a winning tradition.

There have been a few bright spots over the decades, but probably the worst time to have been a Padres fan was during those first few hair-pulling, teeth-grinding seasons when the managers weren't only concerned about the team's survival on the field, but off it as well.

If there is one bright piece of statistical history to take from the Padres first few seasons, it's that at least they were consistent. From 1969 to 1974, the Padres finished in sixth place in the National League West division, never once earning a winning percentage over .389 percent.

Along with poor play on the field came dwindling numbers of fans in seats. Padres owner C. Arnolt Smith began the laborious process of looking for a buyer and soon found Joseph Danzansky, who tendered a respectable offer along with plans to ship the entire franchise to the District of Columbia.

Washington had previously tried its hand at supporting a major league franchise on several occasions, with several incarnations of the Washington Senators and the Washington Nationals. However, none of the clubs had survived the pressures of a few bad seasons and eventually fell into the historical franchise garbage bin. Danzansky had tried to keep the previous Washington Senators in the city—the Senators moved to Texas in 1972 and became the Rangers—and tried to secure a new franchise when the league had expanded, but he failed in all attempts. It was hoped that the purchase of the Padres would finally establish a permanent team in the nation's capital.

The negotiations between Smith and Danzansky had progressed such that new players' uniforms had already been made. Even the Topps baseball card company had produced a series of 1974 cards with the players in San Diego Padres uniforms but with the title Washington National League scrolled across the top.

But in the 11th hour, the San Diego Padres were saved when C. Arnholt Smith decided to sell the Padres to McDonald's co-founder Ray Kroc, who had no interest in moving the team from San Diego. It was a major blow for Major League Baseball's future in Washington, and they had to wait until the 2004 season, when the Montreal Expos folded operations and moved to DC to become the Washington Nationals.

Notable Players

Several outstanding players have played for the Padres at one time or another over the years, and the club has one Hall of Fame player:

Tony Gwynn (right fielder), 1982–2001

In addition, the following Hall of Famers also had short stints with the team:

Dave Winfield (outfielder), 1973–80
Willie McCovey (first base), 1974–76
Rollie Fingers (pitcher), 1977–80
Gaylord Perry (pitcher), 1978–79
Ozzie Smith (shortstop), 1978–81
Dick Williams (manager), 1982–85
Rich "Goose" Gossage (pitcher), 1984–87
Rickey Henderson (outfielder), 1996–97 and 2001

More California Baseball
Fast Facts

- In 1988, Oakland Athletics Jose Canseco became the first major league player to hit 40 home runs and steal 40 bases in the same season.
- Oakland Athletics Jose Canseco and Mark McGwire were known as the "Bash Brothers" for their habit of hitting home runs.
- When the Brooklyn Dodgers made the move to Los Angeles in 1958, legendary radio play-by-play announcer Vin Scully followed the team to sunny California.
- During the 1981 World Series, which pitted the New York Yankees against the Los Angeles Dodgers, Yankee pitcher Goose Gossage beaned Dodgers batter Ron Cey. It was because of this beaning that the major leagues made it mandatory for all batters to wear the double earflap helmet.
- Tommy Lasorda was the longest serving manager in L.A. Dodgers' history, leading the club for 22 seasons. If you count the years that the franchise spent in Brooklyn, then manager Walter Alston leads the club with 23 years as the Dodgers' bench boss.
- The San Diego Padres joined the majors in 1969 along with the new expansion Montreal Expos, Kansas City Royals and Seattle Pilots.
- Ted Williams was born in San Diego on August 30, 1918.
- In the Padres' first home game of the 1974 season, new owner Ray Kroc grabbed the public address system microphone and apologized to fans for the team's poor performance on the field, saying, "I've

never seen such stupid ball playing in my life!" The moment he completed his sentence, a fan darted out onto the field, which incited Kroc to yell, "Throw him in jail!" Ray Kroc is better known as the co-founder of the McDonald's Restaurant franchise.
- Outfielder Darren Lewis played 392 errorless games for the Oakland Athletics and the San Francisco Giants from 1990 to 1994.
- Throughout the history of baseball, there have been many great base stealers: Ty Cobb, Lou Brock, Vince Coleman and many more, but no one was better than Rickey Henderson. The Oakland Athletics outfielder was always ready to steal extra bases and has the records to prove it—Henderson stole a record 130 bases in 1982.

Baseball Hall of Famers from California

Gary Carter (catcher) from Culver City—Montreal Expos (1974–84, 1992), New York Mets (1985–89), San Francisco Giants (1990) and Los Angeles Dodgers (1991). Carter was a three-time Gold Glove Award winner and hit 324 home runs in his 19 years playing in the major leagues. One highlight was a clutch, 10th-inning single in Game 6 of the 1986 World Series that led to a Mets comeback victory and a World Series title. Gary Carter was inducted into the Hall of Fame in 2003.

Frank Chance (first baseman) from Fresno—Chicago Cubs (1898–1912) and New York Yankees (1913–14). Chance was the first baseman in the Tinker-to-Evers-to-Chance double-play combination that was made famous in a 1910 poem. He was a great fielder, hitter and inspirational player-manager. Chance helped the Cubs win four pennants in five years (1906–10) and was given the nickname "The Peerless Leader." In 1906, the Cubs won 116 games—unmatched in major league history. Frank Chance was inducted into the Hall of Fame in 1946.

Joe Cronin (shortstop) from San Francisco—Pittsburgh Pirates (1926–27), Washington Senators (1928–34) and Boston Red Sox (1935–45). Joe Cronin was the American League's All-Star shortstop seven times and MVP in 1930. He had a batting average of .300 or more for eight seasons and also had 100 RBIs or more for eight seasons. Joe Cronin was inducted into the Hall of Fame in 1956.

Joe DiMaggio (center fielder) from Martinez—New York Yankees (1936–42 and 1946–51). Joe DiMaggio is widely regarded as one of baseball's greatest athletes. In 1941, he had a 56 consecutive-game hitting streak that many consider to be the greatest baseball achievement of all time. DiMaggio won three MVP Awards, hit 361 home runs, averaged 118 RBIs per year and retired with a .325 lifetime batting average. Joe DiMaggio was inducted into the Hall of Fame in 1955.

Bobby Doerr (second baseman) from Los Angeles—Boston Red Sox (1937–44 and 1946–51). Bobby Doerr had a .288 career batting average and hit .409 in the 1946 World Series. He had 120 RBIs in 1950 and 100 or more RBIs for six seasons. At one point, Doerr held the American League record for managing 414 chances without an error and would often lead second basemen in the American League in double plays, putouts and assists. He was inducted into the Hall of Fame in 1986.

Don Drysdale (pitcher) from Van Nuys—Brooklyn Dodgers (1956–57) and Los Angeles Dodgers (1958–69). Don Drysdale was a force to be reckoned with from the mound and used brushback pitches and a sidearm fastball to rattle hitters. He holds the National League record for hit batters (154). In 1962, Drysdale won 25 games and the Cy Young Award. In 1968, he set a record of 58 consecutive scoreless innings. Drysdale was also a good hitter. In 1965, he had the only .300 batting average for the Dodgers and hit seven home runs in two separate seasons, tying the National League record. Don Drysdale was inducted into the Hall of Fame in 1984.

Dennis Eckersley (pitcher) from Oakland—Cleveland Indians (1975–77), Boston Red Sox (1978–84 and 1998), Chicago Cubs (1984–86), Oakland A's (1987–95) and St. Louis Cardinals (1996–97). Dennis Eckersley pitched a no-hitter in 1977 and won over 150 games during the first 12 years of his career. And, in the final 12 years of his career, he was credited with almost 400 saves. He helped Oakland to four American League West titles and, in 1992, earned both the Cy Young Award and MVP honors. Eckersley is the only pitcher to record 100 saves and 100 complete games, and from 1988 to 1993, he struck out 458 batters while walking only 51. He was inducted into the Hall of Fame in 2004.

Vernon "Lefty" Gomez (pitcher) from Rodeo—New York Yankees (1930–42) and Washington

Senators (1943). Lefty Gomez had a smoking fastball and a great curve ball. He won 20 or more games four times during the 1930s and helped the Yankees take home seven pennants. Gomez won the pitching Triple Crown in 1934 and 1937 and set a World Series record, winning six games with no losses. He was inducted into the Hall of Fame in 1972.

Joe Gordon (second baseman) from Los Angeles—New York Yankees (1938–43 and 1946) and Cleveland Indians (1947–50). Joe Gordon hit 25 home runs in his rookie season with the Yankees in 1938. In 1942, he had a .322 batting average, won the American League MVP Award and was named to the American League All-Star team nine times. Gordon hit 20 or more home runs in six seasons, had at least 100 RBIs in four seasons and was part of five World Series winning teams. He was inducted into the Hall of Fame in 2009.

Tony Gwynn (outfielder) from Los Angeles—San Diego Padres (1982–2001). Tony Gwynn was a master at finding the hole between the third baseman and the shortstop and had 3141 career hits. He also had a career .338 batting average, won eight batting titles and was one of the first hitters to use video to study his swing. Gwynn won five outfield Gold Glove Awards, stole 319 bases during his career and was selected for the All-Star Game 15 times. He was inducted into the Hall of Fame in 2007.

Chick Hafey (left fielder) from Berkeley—St. Louis Cardinals (1924–31) and Cincinnati Reds (1932–35 and 1937). Chick Hafey was known for hitting powerful line drives. He started having vision problems during his career and had to wear glasses when he played. However, Hafey still managed to tie a National League record with 10 straight hits in the 1929 season, had the best batting average (.349) in the National League in 1931 and batted .329 or better for six consecutive years. He was inducted into the Hall of Fame in 1971.

Harry Heilmann (right fielder and first baseman) from San Francisco—Detroit Tigers (1914, 1916–29) and Cincinnati Reds (1930–31). Harry Heilmann posted a .342 lifetime batting average that ranks third in history among right-handed batters. He won four batting titles between 1921 and 1927 and averaged .394, .403, .393 and .398 for each of those years. Harry Heilmann was inducted into the Hall of Fame in 1952.

Harry Hooper (right fielder) from Bell Station—Boston Red Sox (1909–20) and Chicago White Sox (1921–25). Harry Hooper was a stellar leadoff hitter and outfielder. He's the only player to have been a part of four Red Sox World Championship teams. Hooper earned a civil engineering degree from St. Mary's College in Moraga and was known for being intelligent and well mannered. He holds the Red Sox all-time record for triples (130) and stolen bases (300) and was inducted into the Hall of Fame in 1971.

George Kelly (first baseman) from San Francisco—New York Giants (1915–17 and 1919–26), Pittsburgh Pirates (1917), Cincinnati Reds (1927–30), Chicago Cubs (1930) and Brooklyn Dodgers (1932). George Kelly was a clutch hitter and had a .300 batting average or better for six straight seasons. He also posted over

100 RBIs for four consecutive years and established single-season league records for chances, putouts, assists and double plays by a first baseman. Kelly contributed to four consecutive pennant wins from 1921 to 1924 while with the Giants and was inducted into the Hall of Fame in 1973.

Tony Lazzeri (second baseman) from San Francisco—New York Yankees (1926–37), Chicago Cubs (1938), Brooklyn Dodgers (1939) and New York Giants (1939). Tony Lazzeri was a powerful hitter and was part of six pennant wins. He also recorded a .300 batting average for five seasons and had 100 or more RBIs seven times. In 1936, Lazzeri set an American League single-game record of 11 RBIs, and in 1925, he had 60 home runs and 222 RBIs. He was inducted into the Hall of Fame in 1991.

Bob Lemon (pitcher) from San Bernardino—Cleveland Indians (1941–42 and 1946–58). Bob Lemon started out as an infielder and outfielder, but eight years into it, he switched to pitching. He had seven 20-win seasons over a nine-year period and was a big part of the 1948 and 1954 pennants that Cleveland took home. Lemon went 20–14 in 1948 and 23–7 in 1954. He also became a successful manager and led the Yankees to the world championship in 1978. Bob Lemon was inducted into the Hall of Fame in 1976.

Ernie Lombardi (catcher) from Oakland—Brooklyn Dodgers (1931), Cincinnati Reds (1932–41), Boston Braves (1942) and New York Giants (1943–47). Ernie Lombardi was a strong hitter and, over 17 years, posted a .306 batting average. He hit .300 or better for 10 seasons, was awarded the National League MVP Award in 1938 and batting titles in 1938 and 1942. Ernie Lombardi was inducted into the Hall of Fame in 1986.

Eddie Murray (first baseman) from Los Angeles—Baltimore Orioles (1977–88 and 1996), Los Angeles Dodgers (1989–91 and 1997), New York Mets (1992–93), Cleveland Indians (1994–96) and Anaheim Angels (1997). From the late 1970s through the 1990s, Eddie Murray was one of baseball's most productive batters. When he retired, he was only the third player to have notched both 3000 hits and 500 home runs. Murray is the all-time career RBI leader for switch-hitters and won the Gold Glove Award three times. He was an eight-time All-Star and helped Baltimore bring home a world championship in 1983. Eddie Murray was inducted into the Hall of Fame in 2003.

Tom Seaver (pitcher) from Fresno—New York Mets (1967–77 and 1983), Cincinnati Reds (1977–82), Chicago White Sox (1984–86) and Boston Red Sox (1986). Thomas Seaver was a powerful pitcher who won 311 games with a 2.86 ERA over 20 seasons. He also set a National League record of 3272 strikeouts and had 3640 career strikeouts, including 19 in a single game. Seaver was the National League Rookie of the Year in 1967, was a three-time recipient of the Cy Young Award and was given more opening day starts (16) than any pitcher in history. He was inducted into the Hall of Fame in 1992.

Duke Snider (center fielder) from Los Angeles—Brooklyn Dodgers (1947–57), Los Angeles Dodgers

(1958–62), New York Mets (1963) and San Francisco Giants (1964). Duke Snider was a big hitter in the 1950s, hitting 40 or more homers for five consecutive seasons and, in the 1950s, had the most home runs and RBIs in Major League Baseball. Snider hit four home runs in two different World Series (1952 and 1955) and notched a total of 11 World Series home runs and 26 RBIs. He was inducted into the Hall of Fame in 1980.

Ted Williams (left fielder) from San Diego—Boston Red Sox (1939–42 and 1946–60). Ted Williams is considered to be one of the greatest hitters in baseball history. He was known for taking a scientific approach to hitting and set numerous records even though he missed almost five full seasons while serving during World War II. Williams notched a .406 batting average in 1941, earned two MVPs, six American League batting championships, 521 home runs, a lifetime average of .344 and 17 All-Star game selections in his career. He was inducted into the Hall of Fame in 1966.

Chapter Three

California Hoops

The Basketball State
Pro Hoops Factory

Which state in the U.S. has produced the most pro basketball players? If you guessed Texas, not bad: 124 players in NBA and ABA history come from the Lone Star state. Florida? Nope, only 88 players have been developed in gator country so far. How about Pennsylvania? That's a better guess: 167 pro ballers hail from Pennsylvania, including Kobe Bryant. What's that? New York? Very close! New York State has produced 283 NBA and ABA players to date. Okay, enough guesses (and if Vermont came to mind, you're very cold—the land of maple syrup can claim a grand total of zero players who have played professional hoops).

The answer is, of course, California—so far, 311 NBA and ABA players have hailed from the Golden State.

Notable Californian Hoopsters

Here's a list of a few players you might be familiar with:

Ray Allen has been playing in the NBA since 1996—Milwaukee Bucks (1996–2003), Seattle SuperSonics (2003–07) and Boston Celtics (2007–present). He was born on Castle Air Force Base near Merced and is a nine-time NBA All-Star.

Gilbert Arenas has been playing in the NBA since 2001 (Golden State Warriors 2001–02 and Washington Wizards 2003–present) and attended Grant High School in Valley Glen. He is a three-time NBA All-Star and one of only 20 NBA players to have scored 60 or more points in a game.

Gail Goodrich played in the NBA from 1965 to 1979 for the Los Angeles Lakers (1965–68 and 1970–76), Phoenix Suns (1968–70) and New Orleans Jazz (1977–79). He was born in Los Angeles, went to high school there and played for John Wooden at the University of California, Los Angeles. Goodrich was a five-time NBA All-Star and was inducted into the Basketball Hall of Fame in 1996.

Kevin Johnson played in the NBA from 1987 to 2000 for the Cleveland Cavaliers (1987–88) and Phoenix Suns (1988–98, 2000). He was born in Sacramento, went to Sacramento High School and attended the University of California, Berkeley. Johnson was a three-time NBA All-Star and was elected mayor of Sacramento in 2008.

Reggie Miller played in the NBA from 1987 to 2005 for the Indiana Pacers. He was born in Riverside and went to high school there before attending the University of California, Los Angeles. Miller was a five-time NBA All-Star, is the all-time NBA leader in total three-point field goals made (2560) and scored a three-pointer in 68 consecutive games from November 15, 1996, to April 6, 1997.

Paul Pierce has been playing in the NBA since 1998 with the Boston Celtics. He was born in Oakland and attended Inglewood High School in Inglewood. Pierce is an eight-time NBA All-Star and was the NBA finals MVP in 2008.

Reggie Theus played in the NBA from 1978 to 1991 for the Chicago Bulls (1978–84), Kansas City Kings/Sacramento Kings (1984–88), Atlanta Hawks (1988–89), Orlando Magic (1989–90) and New Jersey Nets (1990–91). He was born in Inglewood and went to Inglewood High School. Theus is a two-time NBA All-Star and one of only seven players in NBA history to score at least 19,000 points and amass 6000 assists. He has been a coach in the NBA since 2007.

Bill Walton played in the NBA from 1974 to 1987 for the Portland Trailblazers (1974–79), San Diego/Los Angeles Clippers (1979–85) and Boston Celtics (1985–87). He was born in La Mesa, went to high school there and played for John Wooden at the University of California, Los Angeles. Walton was a two-time NBA All-Star and was inducted into the Basketball Hall of Fame in 1993.

Jamaal Wilkes played in the NBA from 1974 to 1986 for the Golden State Warriors (1974–77), Los Angeles Lakers (1977–85) and Los Angeles Clippers

(1985–86). He was born in Berkeley, went to high school in Santa Barbara and played for John Wooden at the University of California, Los Angeles. Wilkes was a three-time NBA All-Star and averaged 16.1 points per game in 113 postseason games.

George Yardley was drafted by the Fort Wayne Pistons in 1950 and played in the NBA from 1950 to 1960 (Fort Wayne/Detroit Pistons 1953–59 and Syracuse Nationals 1959–60). He was born in Hollywood, went to Newport Harbor High School in Newport and attended Stanford University in Palo Alto. George Yardley was inducted into the NBA Hall of Fame in 1996.

Los Angeles Lakers

Magic Makes an Announcement

For nearly two decades, Magic Johnson was one of the most recognizable figures in the National Basketball Association (NBA). He won countless awards, championships and personal recognitions for his good works off the court, so in 1991, when Johnson announced in a press conference that he had tested positive for HIV, it came as a great shock to the sporting world and his fans.

In the press conference, he revealed that he had contracted the virus sometime during his playing career by practicing unsafe sex with numerous partners. He also revealed that his wife and unborn child were free from the disease. Because of the HIV-positive diagnosis, Johnson announced that he would retire immediately from the game.

But despite his retirement and diagnosis, Johnson remained ever popular with fans and was voted as a starter for the 1992 NBA All-Star game. Many players protested his inclusion because of fears of contamination should Johnson suffer a cut during the game. But those fears were put aside, and Johnson was crowned MVP of the game with 25 points, nine assists and five rebounds. Johnson attempted a comeback and was set to return to the league, but several players anonymously protested to the league about the dangers of HIV-positive players, thereby forcing Johnson to gracefully bow out of his comeback.

Shaq and Kobe Beef

The same year that the Los Angeles Lakers signed free agent center Shaquille O'Neal, they also acquired the rights to a young, flashy, up-and-comer out of high school named Kobe Bryant. When the two finally played their first season together, they immediately turned the already good Lakers team into a great team.

From 1996 to 2002, the Lakers played intense but frustrating basketball, achieving great things during the regular season but failing to make it deep into the playoffs, and as any sports fan knows, the measure of a great team is its success in the postseason. The worst of those seasons came in 1998–99, when the short-lived experiment of putting Dennis Rodman on the team failed to elicit the proper chemistry. The team managed to make it past the first round against the Houston Rockets, but the Lakers' strange mix of egos was no match for the San Antonio Spurs, and they ended up losing in four straight games. It was the last playoff run by the Lakers in their iconic arena—the Great Western Forum—where past Lakers teams had brought so much glory to the name.

As a result of their poor showing, team owner Jerry Buss brought in six-time NBA champion head coach Phil Jackson at the start of the 1999–2000 season. Jackson was quickly able to tame the various egos on the team, and that year, Shaq and Kobe strong-armed their way through the 2000 playoffs and led the Lakers to the NBA Championship.

But after the euphoria of the 2000 championship had worn off and the team returned for the start of the 2000–01 season, things between Shaq and Kobe began to visibly fall apart. It was a battle of egos on and off the court, but luckily, their personal feuds did not show in the way they played together, and once again, the Lakers were the dominant team in the NBA, winning their second consecutive NBA Championship. Afterward, the two players publicly admitted to the feud, but winning two straight championships seemed to put those feelings on the back burner, at least for the time being.

Battle of Words

The real feud erupted in the 2002–03 season, when the team got off to one of the worst starts in their history, and then Shaq was sidelined with a toe injury. The Lakers managed to pull together enough wins to make the postseason, but they were eliminated in the early rounds of the playoffs.

Then in the summer of 2003 came the rape allegations against Kobe. Following that, just prior to the start of the 2003–04 season, Bryant was absent from training camp because of his legal problems and a knee injury. When asked about Bryant's absence, Shaq said that the whole team was already together and that no one was missing, obviously implying that the team did not need Bryant to win games.

When Bryant finally did join the team for training camp, Shaq commented in the press that Kobe should "stick to being a passer" instead of a scorer until his knee healed. Upset by the comment, Kobe fired back in the media that he did not appreciate the advice from Shaq on how to play guard. Then Shaq retorted again in the press that he could give his advice as he saw fit because the Lakers were "his" team and that if Kobe didn't like it, then he should find another team.

The verbal jabs went back and forth, and the conflict became the media's number-one story over the Lakers' actual performance on the court. Despite the obvious disharmony on the team, the Lakers managed to make it to the NBA finals once again, but they lost in embarrassing fashion to the Detroit Pistons in five games.

End of the Era

At the press conference after the loss, Shaq addressed the uncertainty around the team's future and his place on the team. When Shaq's favorite coach, Jackson, was not offered a contract extension—some said it was because Bryant was upset with Jackson's system—Shaq demanded a trade. O'Neal was eventually traded to the Miami Heat, while Bryant remained with the Lakers.

The feud wasn't as prominent after the trade, but Shaq kept up his criticism of Bryant. At one point,

Shaq was videotaped in a club rapping about his former teammate and saying things like, "Kobe couldn't do it without me," in reference to the Lakers' 2008 loss in the NBA finals to the Boston Celtics, and then saying, "Kobe, tell me how my ass tastes," to which Bryant refused to comment.

The two have since stated that the feud was simply good marketing, but you'd expect, with two big egos on one team, that there would be some friction. After O'Neal's tasteless rap remarks, however, the two players have both been seen publicly supporting one another, and at the 2009 NBA All-Star game, they were awarded a shared MVP title.

Sacramento Kings

Traveling Team

Sacramento is home to the Sacramento Kings NBA team. The franchise started off in Rochester, New York, as a semi-pro team sponsored by Seagrams from 1920 to 1940. After World War II, the team became part of the National Basketball League and was known as the Rochester Royals from 1945 to 1957. The Royals moved to Cincinnati from 1957 to 1972, and then on to Kansas City. However, since the Kansas City Royals were already a baseball team there, they changed their name to the Kansas City-Omaha Kings from 1972 to 1975 and then, from 1975 to 1985, were known as the Kansas City Kings.

The franchise relocated to Sacramento for the 1985–86 season, but the early years in California were a bit rough for the Kings. The team had strong fan support and won over 60 percent of their home games, but they went 1–40 on the road during the 1990–91 season. The Kings managed to make the NBA playoffs in 1996—thanks in large part to the contributions of six-time NBA All-Star shooting guard, Mitch Richmond—but had trouble achieving any success in the postseason.

The Maloof family—owners of The Palms hotel and casino in Las Vegas, Nevada, among other interests—acquired a minority interest in the Kings in 1998 and took majority control in 1999. After the change in ownership, the Sacramento Kings won two consecutive NBA division titles in 2002 and 2003.

In 2006, the Maloofs caused quite a stir in Sacramento when they announced their plans to build a new basketball arena in downtown Sacramento, but they didn't want to cover the majority of the expenses. So they successfully lobbied for a tax-increase proposal to be included on the fall election ballots—the quarter-cent sales tax hike was designed to raise $1.2 billion over the next 15 years in order to finance the arena. Voters strongly opposed the proposal.

As a result, some believe that the team could relocate yet again. Anaheim, San Jose, Las Vegas, Seattle and Kansas City have all been rumored as potential new homes for the Kings franchise.

Los Angeles Clippers

Clippers Jokes

The Los Angeles Clippers have been so bad for so many years that jokes about their awful play on the court have naturally made their way into popular culture. Here are just a few of the thousands of Clippers jokes to choose from (with my apologies to Clippers fans, if you're out there...):

Q: Why are the Los Angeles Clippers like the U.S. Postal Service?

A: They both wear uniforms and fail to deliver.

Q: What do the Los Angeles Clippers and Billy Graham have in common?

A: They both can make 20,000 people stand up and yell, "Jesus Christ!"

Q: What do you call a Los Angeles Clipper with an NBA championship?

A: A myth.

Q: What do the Los Angeles Clippers and possums have in common?

A: Both play dead at home and get killed on the road.

Q: Where is the safest place to leave your naked wife?

A: With the Clippers; they can't score.

Q: What do you call a bunch of millionaires sitting around a TV watching the NBA playoffs?

A: The Clippers.

Good Dog

While attending a Los Angeles Clippers game, a guy notices another guy with a dog at his side. To his amazement, when the Clippers score, the dog does a flip. Again they score, and again the dog does a flip. This goes on three or four times until the guy finally can't stand it any more and has to ask why the dog does a flip every time the team scores.

So, he gets up and goes over to the guy with the dog and says, "Excuse me sir, I have a question about your dog. I noticed that every time the Clippers score a basket, your dog does a flip. Why?"

The man replies, "I know it's weird, but I have no explanation for why he does it."

The other man then asks the obvious question, "So what does he do when the Clippers win a game?"

The guy with the dog replies without hesitation, "I don't know. I've only had him for 15 years."

First Grade Smarts

A first grade teacher explains to her class that she is a Los Angeles Clippers fan. She then asks her students to raise their hands if they are Clippers fans as well. All of their hands fly into the air, except for one little boy's.

"Why didn't you raise your hand?" the teacher asks him.

"Because I'm not a Clippers fan," replies the boy.

"Then," asks the teacher, "what are you?"

"I'm a proud Sacramento Kings fan," the boy replies.

The teacher gets a little red in the face and asks the little boy, "Why are you a Kings fan?"

"Well, my mom and dad are Kings fans, so I'm a Kings fan, too," he responds.

The teacher, now angry, says, "That's no reason to be a Kings fan. What if your mom was a meth junkie and your dad was retarded. What would you be then?"

The little boy sits up straight and says, "A Clippers fan!"

More California Basketball
Bruins and Wooden

Legendary basketball coach, John Wooden, accepted the head coach job for the University of California, Los Angeles (UCLA) men's basketball team in 1948. However, it's a little-known fact that UCLA was actually his second choice for a coaching position that year. His first choice was with the University of Minnesota Golden Gophers, but bad weather prevented the University of Minnesota from being able to offer him the job via phone as scheduled, so he pulled the trigger with UCLA. By the time the U of M officials finally got through to Wooden, he had already given his word to the Bruins, so he turned down their offer and headed west.

Wooden made an immediate impact at UCLA. The season before he arrived, the Bruins had a losing season of 12–13. In Wooden's first year, the Bruins finished with a record of 22–7 and were Pacific Coast Conference Southern Division champs. It was the most wins the team had ever had since they were originally formed in 1919. In his second season at UCLA, Wooden coached the team to a 24–7 record, winning a second Southern Division championship and the Pacific Coast Conference.

Despite his early success with the Bruins, Wooden and his wife were apparently not very happy living in Los Angeles, and he contemplated taking a job at Purdue. However, he had signed a three-year contract in 1948 and ultimately decided that he simply couldn't break his word.

UCLA had a 17-game winning streak during the 1955–56 season, and Wooden coached the team to its first undefeated Pacific Coast Conference title. Shortly thereafter, things stalled a bit for the Bruins when a probation was imposed on all UCLA sports following a scandal regarding illegal payments made to Bruins football players. The University of Southern California, University of California, Berkeley, and Stanford were also found guilty of the same allegations.

However, when the probation was over, Wooden was able to get the team back on track, and in 1962, the Bruins made their first of what would be 12 "Final Four" appearances from 1962 to 1975. A couple of seasons later, Wooden's assistant coach, Jerry Norman, talked Wooden into marrying their small-sized players and fast-paced offense with a zone-press defense. This change increased their scoring significantly, and in 1964, the Bruins won their first of what would be 10 NCAA championships from 1964 to 1975.

John Wooden coached his last game at UCLA's Pauley Pavilion on March 1, 1975, and retired at the end of that season. Wooden was named NCAA College Basketball's "Coach of the Year" in 1964, 1967, 1969, 1970, 1971, 1972 and 1973, and was known as the "Wizard of Westwood," leading UCLA to 620 wins in his 27 seasons there. Besides the unprecedented and unrivaled 10 NCAA titles won during his last 12 seasons at UCLA—seven in a row from 1967 to 1973—the Bruins also had a record winning streak of 88 games, four perfect 30–0 seasons and set a record of 98 straight wins at home.

Wooden reportedly turned down an offer to coach the Los Angeles Lakers while he was at UCLA and, in 1973, he became the first person to be honored as both a player and a coach in the Basketball Hall of Fame. John Wooden died at the age of 99 on June 4, 2010, in Los Angeles.

Fast Facts

- The Los Angeles Clippers, along with the Memphis Grizzlies and the Charlotte Bobcats, are the only teams never to have won an NBA championship, a conference championship or a division championship in their franchise's history.
- The Los Angeles Clippers began their franchise history as the Buffalo Braves, then they were called the San Diego Clippers and, in 1984, became the Los Angeles Clippers.
- Both the Los Angeles Lakers and the Clippers share the Staples Center as their home arena.
- The Los Angeles Lakers have won the NBA championship 16 times—only the Boston Celtics have won it more, with 17 titles.
- The Sacramento Kings franchise has moved around the NBA often—they started out as the Rochester Royals (1945–57), became the Cincinnati Royals (1957–72), then the Kansas City-Omaha Kings (1972–75) and the Kansas City Kings (1975–85), before finally settling in Sacramento in 1985.

- The Sacramento Kings mascot is named "Slamson the Lion." Before him, the Kings mascot was "The Gorilla."
- The Golden State Warriors franchise began as the Philadelphia Warriors, for which a young Wilt Chamberlain scored 100 points in a single game.
- Before moving to Oakland to become the Golden State Warriors, the franchise was based in San Francisco from 1962 to 1971, where they were called the Warriors as well.
- Manute Bol, originally from Sudan, played for the Golden State Warriors from 1988 to 1990 and again in 1994. At seven feet, seven inches, he is the tallest player to ever play in the NBA, ranks first in career blocks per 48 minutes (8.6), second in career blocks per game average (3.34), 14th in total blocked shots (2086) and is the only player in NBA history to block more shots than points scored, blocking 2086 shots and scoring 1599 points.
- The Golden State Warriors have only won one NBA championship, in 1975.

Chapter Four

Hockey in California?

Los Angeles Kings
The Gretzky Trade

Wayne Gretzky was the greatest player in the history of the game. With the Edmonton Oilers, he established countless records and accomplished many great things after joining the NHL in 1979. It was thought impossible that any general manager or owner in his right mind would want to get rid of a dynamic player of Gretzky's caliber. After all, Gretzky was responsible for bringing the Stanley Cup to Edmonton four times and had made the team into the most powerful club in the league.

By 1988, Gretzky was the king of hockey and could do no wrong in the eyes of all Edmonton Oilers fans. The idea of Gretzky leaving the club never entered people's mind. He was an Oiler and that was final. Gretzky was Canada's golden boy and no one wanted to share.

After the 1988 Stanley Cup victory celebrations had died down and the players relaxed over the summer, strange rumors began swirling around the NHL that the Oilers were on the verge of making a major multi-player trade that could possibly involve Gretzky. Most fans in the city simply dismissed the rumors as lies and fabrications. Rumors always tended to creep into the hockey world during the off-season, but they were more the product of bored sports writers than the stirrings of truth.

But this time was different—this story had legs. And when Oilers management called an emergency press conference on August 9, 1988, most of the hockey world was caught off guard.

The Announcement

At the press conference, the room fell eerily silent as Oilers management walked in and took their seats. With a rather sedate look on his face, Oilers owner Peter Pocklington took his seat, shuffled a few papers, took a deep breath and uttered the words that broke millions of hearts.

"Wayne Gretzky has been traded to the Los Angeles Kings," he said as flashbulbs illuminated the room.

What no one in that room that day knew was that Pocklington and charismatic Kings owner Bruce McNall had signed the deal two weeks earlier. The reason they had not told the world their little secret was that the Oilers' season ticket drive was on and any news of Gretzky leaving the team surely would have affected sales.

The trade was monumental not just for the fact the Gretzky was leaving for the warmer climes of Southern California, but that a slew of other players were also involved in the deal. Along with Gretzky, the Oilers sent enforcer Marty McSorley and Mike Krushelnyski to Los Angeles in return for Jimmy Carson and Martin Gelinas. The Oilers also received several of the Kings' first-round draft picks in 1989, 1991 and 1993, as well as a chunk of change reported to be in the area of $15 million.

After Pocklington finished his earth-shattering announcement, it was time for Gretzky to address the media. There were no visible signs of happiness on his face as he sat down and shuffled closer to the microphone. Taking a couple of breaths, Gretzky proceeded to confirm the news that nobody wanted to hear.

"For the benefit of Wayne Gretzky, my new wife and our expected child in the new year, it would be for the benefit of everyone involved to let me play for the Los Angeles Kings," said Gretzky, choking back tears. "I promised Mess [Mark Messier] I wouldn't do this."

A sudden ripple of collective shock ran across Canada as the news sank in. The boy from Brantford, Ontario, whom the country had watched grow into one of the greatest hockey players in the world, had just been handed over to a U.S. team without so much as a fight.

Edmonton Sun journalist Terry Jones best summed up the feelings of all Canadians when he wrote, "The emotions we're dealing with here are not unlike those of a death in the family. A death not by natural causes."

Welcome to Los Angeles

In contrast to the sadness caused by the announcement in Edmonton, things looked a lot brighter from the Kings' perspective. The welcoming party at the Kings' headquarters was a decidedly more festive affair than the goodbyes in Edmonton. Gretzky was all smiles when Bruce McNall handed him his iconic number 99 jersey in Kings black and silver, officially welcoming him into the California fold.

Although it might not have been apparent then, the Gretzky trade was more than just a transfer of players from one team to another. When a player of Gretzky's caliber and stature is brought into a market where football and basketball reign supreme, his arrival can change the game. He brought a renewed interest in hockey to California, which was great news for a team struggling to put fans in seats. Practically overnight, the Los Angeles Kings became the hottest ticket in town. Gretzky was the new star in a town that worshipped stars.

Gretzky in LA

At the start of the season before Gretzky's arrival, the Kings had only managed to sell 4500 season tickets. But by the opening day of the new Gretzky-era, the Kings had sold 13,000 season tickets. The team now not only attracted regular sports fans, but at nearly every home game, you could find celebrities like Jack Nicholson, Kurt Russell and Goldie Hawn cheering the Kings along.

Not only was Gretzky good for the Kings' bottom line, but the team on the ice also saw an upswing in their standings. The year before Gretzky arrived, the Kings had finished the season with just 68 points and had scored only 318 goals. But with Gretzky in their ranks, the Kings improved their standing, finished with 91 points, scored 376 goals and finally made it out of the first round of the playoffs for the first time since 1982. The players flanking Gretzky on the left and right wings had banner years under the Great One's tutelage. Linemate Bernie Nicholls had previously been a respectable goal scorer with a career-high 46 goals in one season, but the year of Gretzky's arrival saw his scoring output increase to 70 goals.

The Gretzky effect was not just confined to the ice arena. Selling hockey in the southern United States was something that the NHL had always set its mind on, but it was never able to create a lasting foothold. Of the teams that previously tried to stake out a fan base in the southern U.S., most have either failed or just barely managed to keep their team solvent. Hockey is a winter sport of ice and snow. In the Southern States, most people have never seen snow, let alone heard of this crazy game Canadians played called "hockey." What Gretzky accomplished was to get a whole new generation of kids interested in the game. Where before there were no hockey programs for kids, suddenly communities began to build the infrastructure to support the development of the game.

At the NHL level, Gretzky's impact on the game could be seen as well. With the new interest in hockey, the NHL finally felt comfortable bringing in more franchises. By 1994, the list of southern-based U.S. franchises had expanded to include the San Jose Sharks, the Anaheim Mighty Ducks, the Dallas Stars, the Tampa Bay Lightning and the Florida Panthers. Within another five years, the NHL added the Phoenix Coyotes, the Carolina

Hurricanes and the Colorado Avalanche to the growing list of NHL teams. And while Gretzky cannot be credited completely with the expansion of hockey into the southern states, his immediate success in Los Angeles showed the league that it was possible to thrive in non-traditional markets.

There will always be people who say that Gretzky leaving Edmonton sounded the death knell for Canadian franchises, but no one can argue against the positive effect that Gretzky had in promoting hockey in the U.S. The only icing-on-the-cake scenario would have been for Gretzky and the Kings to bring the Stanley Cup to Los Angeles, but they were never able to claim the grand prize, even though they came very close.

802 Career Goals

On October 15, 1989, Los Angeles Kings centerman Wayne Gretzky picked up an assist in the first period of a game against his former team, the Edmonton Oilers, to tie Gordie Howe's record 1850 career points. Then, in that same game, Gretzky scored the overtime goal to not only win the game but become the sole leader in the NHL for total career points. It was a glorious moment for Gretzky, who had idolized Howe growing up, but he had another one of Howe's records still in his sights: total career goals. Everyone knew the day would eventually come—it was just a matter of when.

He would have to wait a few more years, but that day finally happened on March 23, 1994, when the Los Angeles Kings played the Vancouver Canucks before a crowd of over 16,000 packed into the Great

Western Forum. Two days earlier, Gretzky had scored two goals in a game against the San Jose Sharks and knew that the magic 802 was around the corner.

"This one's pretty special," said Gretzky of his 801st career goal. "I'm just grateful that I had an opportunity." What took the 33-year-old Gretzky 15 seasons to accomplish had taken Howe 26 years. "It's kind of funny to say, but my first feeling about the goal was that it tied the game. Then I thought about it being number 801."

But everyone was waiting for the record breaker, and that moment came in the second period of the game against the Canucks when Luc Robitaille started the rush up ice with Marty McSorley and Gretzky not far behind. Robitaille carried the puck into the Vancouver zone and passed it to Gretzky, who had McSorley with him on a two-on-one. Gretzky hit McSorley with a pass, and though McSorley could have taken the shot, he passed it back to Gretzky, who shoveled it in past netminder Kirk Maclean for his 802nd career goal. "When I got the puck back, I saw the whole net," said Gretzky after the game. "I couldn't believe I saw it."

In an unprecedented move, the game was stopped for 10 minutes to honor the momentous occasion with a brief ceremony at center ice. Despite all the records and Stanley Cup wins, Gretzky will always remember that moment as one of the greatest of his career. NHL commissioner Gary Bettman put it well when he said to the crowd, "You have always been the 'Great One,' but tonight you are the greatest."

Despite all the attention focused on Gretzky, the Vancouver Canucks actually won the game with a final score of 6–3.

Anaheim Ducks
Disney Gets a Hockey Team

Before Wayne Gretzky arrived in California, having more than one hockey team in the Golden State seemed a highly unlikely prospect. But that was only until the city of Anaheim began construction of a $100 million, state-of-the-art arena. The city planners used the *Field of Dreams* philosophy—"If you build it, they will come"—in the hopes of making Anaheim the destination for another professional sports team.

What was once a small town had grown into a major metropolis and was known worldwide as the home of Disneyland. It was hoped that, once a building was in place, the proper business interests would step forward and bring an NHL team to the city. For a few sleepless months, the mayor of Anaheim looked over at his empty white elephant and wondered if the building had been a major mistake, but a savior quickly stepped in to save the day.

The most recognizable company in all of California had expressed interest in starting an NHL franchise in the city. Disney CEO Michael Eisner was already a huge hockey fan and had just released a popular family-oriented film called *The Mighty Ducks,* starring Emilio Estevez, which had pulled in over $50 million at the box office.

Eisner's next step was to speak to Los Angeles Kings owner Bruce McNall on the viability of hockey in California, and after receiving his positive reviews, the Disney Corporation put in the offer to start a franchise. Under the watchful eye of the new NHL commissioner, Gary Bettman, Anaheim and South Florida were handed the rights to start up their respective hockey teams.

Eisner responded to the news with great enthusiasm and hinted at potential future business opportunities. "There's great growth in hockey. In the way hockey is shot [on television], we can be creative in creating stars. We do that in the movie business," said Eisner.

Eisner's business acumen for cross-pollinating Disney products encroached heavily on the company's new acquisition when, much to the dismay of hockey purists everywhere, the new NHL team was named the Mighty Ducks of Anaheim. To make matters even worse, the Mighty Ducks were outfitted in purple, sea green and white uniforms, complete with a picture of a goalie mask in the shape of a cartoon duck. This was also to be the face of their new mascot, Wild Wing.

Ducks on Ice

Despite the obvious groan factor that accompanied the naming and outfitting of the team, the Mighty Ducks were a serious club, and they showed serious intentions when they hired experienced hockey man Jack Ferreira as general manager and former Quebec Nordiques general manager Pierre Gauthier as his assistant. Ron Wilson, an assistant coach with the Vancouver Canucks, was promoted as the Ducks' bench boss, and the team secured its scoring future by drafting Paul Kariya in the 1993 Entry Draft.

On September 18, 1993, the Mighty Ducks of Anaheim played their first exhibition game against the Pittsburgh Penguins. A sellout crowd of over 16,000 people greeted the new team, a good omen for the expansion franchise. On top of the first sellout crowd, the Ducks had sold over 12,000 season tickets and had booked over 40 luxury boxes in the new Arrowhead Pond (the new name given to the already-built Anaheim arena). It was so named after its sponsor, the Arrowhead Mountain Spring Water company, decided to have "Pond" attached to its name, not arena, or rink, or center, but pond, since ducks swim on ponds. Ugh, we get it. Luckily, the name has since been changed to the Honda Center.

On the ice, the team was about what everyone expected: mediocre. But with young talent like Paul Kariya and veteran presence from guys like Stu Grimson, the Ducks finished the 1993–94 season with 71 points. Not good enough for the playoffs, but good enough to finish ahead of the Los Angeles Kings.

The Ducks Come Close

The 2003 playoffs seemed like it would finally be the Ducks' year. After a decent regular season, the team started the playoffs against the 2002 defending Cup champions, the Detroit Red Wings, and upset them in an unexpected four-game sweep. It was that series that announced to the rest of the league that the Anaheim Ducks were serious contenders. Then they made it past Dallas and Minnesota to play in the Stanley Cup finals for the first time in franchise history.

The Ducks were an excellent team up front, but the main reason they had made it so far was between the pipes. Goaltender Jean-Sebastien Giguere had been playing like a man possessed in net and was making one incredible save after another to keep his team in the run for the Cup. But the Ducks were up against the New Jersey Devils in the final.

The Devils were no strangers to success in the Stanley Cup finals and had a host of players on their team with enough playoff experience to get them through the tough patches of a series, not to mention they also had the Vezina Trophy–winning goaltender Martin Brodeur to help them out. Although the Devils would take the first two games in New Jersey by a score of 3–0, Anaheim would roar back with two overtime wins thanks to the solid performance of Giguere.

The series eventually went to a seventh and deciding game, in which the Devils pulled off another 3–0 win to seal the Stanley Cup victory. The Anaheim goaltender did everything he could to stop the Devils' onslaught short of scoring a goal himself. For his Herculean efforts, Giguere was just one of a few players to ever receive the Conn Smythe Trophy—given to the playoffs' most valuable player—but not win the Stanley Cup.

Ducks fans will surely remember the utter look of devastation on Giguere's face as he grudgingly accepted the trophy from league commissioner Gary Bettman. It was the face of a boy who had just lost the chance to make his dreams come true. The Ducks' Cinderella season had ended, but the new season was just a few months away.

Retooling the Team

Over the next few seasons, Ducks general manager Brian Burke set out to secure a lineup of players that combined grit and toughness with finesse and goal scoring. In 2005, he brought in defenseman Scott Niedermayer from the New Jersey Devils and traded away high-priced Russian forward Sergei Fedorov in return for François Beauchemin and Tyler Wright. The emergence of homegrown players like Corey Perry and Ryan Getzlaf also elevated the Ducks to a new level that saw them emerge as a dominant force in the league. The most significant addition to the lineup came during the 2006–07 season, when a disgruntled Chris Pronger left the Edmonton Oilers to join the Ducks. With that addition to the lineup, many put the Ducks on their list of favorites to win the Stanley Cup.

However, as everyone in the hockey world will tell you, nothing is a given. You can add the greatest players in the world to a team and still get terrible results (just ask the New York Rangers). Good hockey is all about good chemistry, and as the 2006–07 season got underway, all eyes were on Brian Burke's creation to see they if could win games.

The Ducks answered all expectations by starting off the season with 12 straight wins. All the lines worked hard throughout the season, and the hockey gods ensured that everyone on the team stayed healthy. By the end of the season, and for the first time in franchise history, the Ducks won the Pacific Division title with a record of 48–20–14 for a total of 110 points.

The 2007 Playoffs

Although the Detroit Red Wings and the Buffalo Sabres finished the regular season with more points, the Ducks were looked on as one of the favorites to make it deep into the playoffs. In the first round, the Ducks faced off against the Minnesota Wild. This was only the second time the Wild had made it into the playoffs in their history, and for the second time, it would be the Anaheim Ducks that eliminated them from contention. Ducks goaltender IIya Bryzgalov started the series because Jean-Sebastien Giguere was tending to his wife and their newborn son. But the switch of netminders did nothing to slow the Ducks' advance. Although the Wild won one game, Giguere returned to the Ducks lineup for Game 5 and helped send Minnesota to the golf course with a 4–1 victory.

Having finished off the Wild so quickly, the Ducks got to sit back and watch while their next opponents, the Vancouver Canucks, battled it out in a hard-fought seven-game series against the Dallas Stars. When Vancouver finally advanced to the next round to meet the Ducks, the Canucks looked a little worn out on the ice compared with the well-rested team from Anaheim, and it showed as the Canucks lost the opening game of the series 5–1. Vancouver managed to pull off an overtime victory in Game 2, but that was all they could muster. The Ducks won the series in five games to move on to face the top team in the West: the Detroit Red Wings.

The Anaheim–Detroit series was the proving ground for the Ducks. If they could put up a fight against the Red Wings, they would surely be the favorites to win the Cup. The Red Wings had not made it into the Conference finals since their last Cup win in 2002, and they were also eager to prove that they still had the depth and talent to win the Cup. But the Ducks' Giguere still had that 2003 loss etched in the back of his mind and wanted to rid himself of that memory and the bad taste it left.

Game 1 could have gone to either team as both battled hard in a tight defensive affair. The Red Wings, though, got all the lucky bounces and scored two goals off deflections in front of Giguere's net that left him with no chance of stopping the puck. The Ducks only managed to slip one goal by Dominik Hasek as the Red Wings ended up taking the first game of the series by a final score of 2–1.

The Niedermayer brothers stole the show in Game 2 as Rob opened up the scoring for the Ducks and Scott scored the winner in overtime to help the Ducks even the series with a 4–3 victory. Game 3, however, was not a good one for Ducks fans. Coming back to the Honda Center, the team hoped to use the momentum from their Game 2 overtime win, but things got off to a bad start. The Ducks could not get a single puck past Hasek and lost the game 5–0.

As bad as that news was, it was even worse when Brian Burke received a call from Director of Hockey Operations Colin Campbell about a vicious hit from behind that Chris Pronger had delivered on the Red

Wings' Tomas Holmstrom. The hit in question did not receive a penalty during the game, but when the league reviewed the tapes and saw Pronger hit Holmstrom from behind, sending him into the boards face first, the league had no choice but to hand out a one-game suspension. The loss of one of their best players was a huge blow for the Ducks, and they all had to step up their game in order to fill the hole Pronger left.

Luckily, in Game 4, the Ducks responded with one of their most complete games of the entire season and handed the Red Wings a series-crushing loss with a score of 5–3. Responding with such a strong victory proved that the Ducks were not riding the tails of one single player and had the talent to take them all the way to finals. The Ducks then finished off the Red Wings with two straight wins to end the series in six games, and it was off into the Stanley Cup finals, this time against the Ottawa Senators.

Led by a top line of Dany Heatley, Daniel Alfredsson and Jason Spezza, the Ottawa Senators were by no means easy pushovers. They had defeated the Pittsburgh Penguins, taken out both the top-seeded New Jersey Devils and the Buffalo Sabres in five-game sweeps and were being backstopped by brilliant performances from goaltender Ray Emery. Most of the attention prior to the start of the series was all about putting Ottawa up on a hockey pedestal, claiming the Senators were Canada's team to win the Cup—the last time a Canadian team had won the Cup was in 1993, when the Montreal Canadiens beat the Los Angeles

Kings. This series would also mark the return of the Senators head coach Bryan Murray, who in 2003 was the general manager of the Ducks when they lost in the finals to the Detroit Red Wings.

For the start of the series, the Ducks found themselves playing before a receptive home crowd at the Honda Center. California governor Arnold Schwarzenegger was on hand to take in the game and dropped the puck in the opening ceremonial face-off. It had all the markings of a great series seeing as both teams could score, and each had excellent goaltending.

The Senators quickly quieted down the Honda Center crowd as Mike Fisher scored the series' first goal just 1:38 into the game on a power play. Although Ottawa had broken the ice in the opening minutes, it was the Ducks that dominated the early play, and just about nine minutes later, winger Andy Macdonald scored the tying goal at even strength. Throughout the rest of the first period, the Senators were on their heels trying to keep the Ducks from entering their zone and only managed three shots by the time the buzzer sounded.

The Senators scored the only goal of the second period on another power play, but the Ducks continued to dictate the overall game. In the third period, Ryan Getzlaf tied up the game early, and then Travis Moen scored the game winner with just under three minutes on the clock. Dany Heatley did not look his normal self throughout much of the game, and it was later revealed that he had suffered an injury from a Chris Pronger crosscheck.

Game 2 was all about defense and goaltending, but Giguere came out on top over Emery as the Ducks took a 2–0 series lead on the strength of a goal from Samuel Pahlsson late in the third period. The series then switched over to Ottawa, where the Senators managed to win one game but lost the second to go down 3–1 in the series.

It was do-or-die time for the Senators in Game 5 back in Anaheim, but the Senators just didn't have the system figured out to beat the Ducks. Giguere was solid in net when he had to be, and the Ducks' forwards potted six goals to lead their team to a 6–2 victory and the Stanley Cup, a sweet redemption for their 2003 finals loss.

This was the first Stanley Cup win for the franchise, the first for California and the first for Giguere. Ducks defenseman Scott Niedermayer was named the MVP. The Ducks' win marked the first time since the Victoria Cougars won the Cup in 1925 that a West Coast team had won the Stanley Cup. It also marked the first time that two expansion teams from the early 1990s played each other in the final.

More California Hockey

Mighty Ducks Movie Plot Synopsis

Gordon Bombay, a hotshot lawyer, is haunted by memories of his childhood when, as the star player on his championship hockey team, he missed the winning goal in a shootout, thereby losing the game and the approval of his coach. After being charged for drunk driving, the court orders him to coach a peewee hockey team, the worst in the league, and Gordon is at first reluctant. However, he eventually gains the respect of the kids and teaches them how to win, gaining a sponsor on the way and naming the team the Mighty Ducks. In the finals, they face off against Gordon's old team, still coached by his former coach, giving Gordon a chance to face his old ghosts.

Fast Facts

- Although many Canadians called the Ottawa Senators "Canada's team" during the 2007 Stanley Cup run, there were more Canadian-born players on the Ducks team than on the Senators.
- Teemu Selanne was the Anaheim Ducks' leading scorer, with 351 goals and 391 assists, as of the end of the 2009–10 season.
- In 1970, Charles Finley, owner of the Oakland Athletics baseball team, purchased the California Golden Seals hockey club after the previous owners declared bankruptcy and the team was left without management.
- The Oakland Seals only managed to make it into the playoff twice in franchise history, in 1969 and 1970, and they lost both times in the opening rounds.
- In one of the most lopsided deals in NHL history, the California Golden Seals traded Francois Lacombe and their first-round draft pick in the 1971 NHL Entry Draft to the Montreal Canadiens in return for the Canadiens' 1970 first-round draft pick, Ernie Hicke, and some money. None of the players the Seals received turned out to be NHL caliber, while the Canadiens used the number-one draft pick to select future Hall of Famer and Montreal legend Guy Lafleur.

Chapter Five

Beautiful Game, Beautiful State

Soccer

The Sports Bra Incident

On July 10, 1999, the Women's World Cup Final between the United States and China was played at the Rose Bowl in Pasadena. This was the best-attended women's sports event in history, with an official attendance of 90,185 as well as worldwide television coverage. The game was still scoreless after extra time and came down to a penalty shootout.

After scoring the fifth kick, which gave the United States the win over China in that final game, Brandi Chastain stripped off her jersey and fell to her knees with clenched fists—obviously ecstatic. In doing so, she bared her sports bra to the world. No big deal, right?

Well, this image was reproduced by media outlets all around the world and was featured on the covers of major publications such as *Time, Newsweek* and *Sports Illustrated*. Chastain described the moment as "Momentary insanity, nothing more and nothing less. I wasn't thinking about anything. I thought, 'This is the greatest moment of my life on the soccer field.'"

The Career of Brandi Chastain

Brandi Chastain was born in San Jose in 1968 and helped her high school team, Archbishop Mitty High School, to three section championships. In 1986, Brandi was awarded the Soccer America Freshmen Player of the Year award at the University of California, Berkeley. Chastain sat out the 1987 and 1988 seasons after having reconstructive surgery on both knees, and then she transferred to Santa Clara University (SCU) in 1989.

While with the SCU Broncos, she helped them make two Final Four NCAA appearances in 1989 and 1990. In 1988, Brandi made her debut representing the U.S. in a game against Japan. And, in 1991, she came off the bench as a forward to score five consecutive goals in a 12–0 win over Mexico, and Team USA went on to win the World Cup that year in China. Chastain played for the U.S. National Team off and on from 1988 to 2004 and has also had a successful professional playing and commentating career.

NCAA

Collegiate soccer is alive and well in California. From 1966 to 2006, 23 California NCAA Division 1 men's soccer teams made it to the national championships, and 11 of those teams pulled out a 'W.' On the women's side, a team from California has played in the NCAA Division 1 National Championship game in seven of the last 10 years (2000–09).

University of San Francisco

It's a little-known fact that, from 1966 to 1980, the University of San Francisco (USF) was an NCAA Division 1 men's soccer powerhouse. The USF Dons played for the national championship in seven of those 15 years and pulled out a win in 1966, 1975, 1977, 1978* and 1980 (*won 2–0 over Indiana but were later disqualified for having an ineligible player).

During that span, their coach was Steve Negoesco, the first coach in NCAA history to surpass 500 career victories. In his fifth season as coach, Negoesco guided the Dons to their first NCAA championship in 1966. The majority of the players on the team were native San Franciscans, who already had a connection with Negoesco.

In an interview, Negoesco said, "To think that a school having three tuition waivers could win a national championship against the eastern and midwestern teams was unheard of, but that's exactly what we did and that was a big, big accomplishment. Most of the kids that I had, I raised them right here in San Francisco. They were my former players from my youth teams that decided to come to USF because I was at USF."

Steve Negoesco retired in 2000 after 778 matches, 540 victories and 34 winning seasons. Thirty of the players he coached were named All-American players by the National Soccer Coaches Association of America (NSCAA) and seven played in the Olympics. Negoesco is regarded as one of the founding fathers of youth soccer in the San Francisco Bay Area.

Chapter Six

Country Club Livin'

Golf

Tiger Woods

"Phenom" is an adjective you hear a lot when Tiger Wood is described. However, he wasn't born with a great swing—it's been developed through a lifetime of dedication and training.

Eldrick Tont "Tiger" Woods was born on December 30, 1975, in Cypress, California. His father, Earl, introduced Tiger to the sport of golf before he could even walk. In fact, he gave Tiger his first metal putter when he was seven months old. Earl was a teacher, coach, former athlete and confessed "golf addict." He was intensely focused on training Tiger, and when Tiger was very young, his father used to set the boy up in a high chair in the garage, and Tiger would watch his dad hit balls into a net for hours at a time.

Before the age of two, Tiger was at the golf course regularly, playing and practicing. He devoted countless hours to developing his golf skill throughout childhood, and both he and his father always credited "hard work" for Tiger's achievements. He went on to have a successful amateur career and played collegiate golf at Stanford University, for two years before turning pro in 1996.

Tiger is now one of the most successful professional golfers in history, one of the most recognizable athletes in the world and has been a catalyst for the sport's popularity. In addition, according to *Forbes*, Tiger is the "richest sportsman in the world," having earned over $1 billion in prize money and endorsement deals thus far.

In 2004, Tiger married Elin Nordegren, a former model from Sweden, and they have two children together—daughter Sam and son Charlie. Tiger's personal life has been under intense scrutiny since November 2009, when news got out that Woods was having extramarital affairs. Media pressure increased after over a dozen women claimed that they had affairs with Tiger, and in December 2009, he released a statement, admitting to infidelity, offering an apology and announcing an indefinite hiatus from professional golf.

A day after the statement was issued, several companies indicated they were reconsidering endorsement deals with Tiger, and a few ended up distancing themselves once it was clear that his clean-cut, nice-guy, marketable image was tarnished forever. Although many believe that the bulk of his fan base doesn't truly care about his personal life, a December 2009 study estimated that his brief absence from the game resulted in a loss of between $5 and $12 billion for shareholders of the corporations that sponsored Tiger.

On February 19, 2010, Woods admitted that he had been unfaithful to his wife and said that he used to believe he was entitled to do whatever he wanted to because his success meant that "normal" rules didn't apply to him. He said he realizes now that he was wrong to have had extramarital affairs and apologized to his family, friends, fans, and business partners for the grief caused by his irresponsible behavior.

Tiger returned to competitive golf in April 2010, and later that month, the *National Enquirer* reported that Woods had confessed to his wife that he'd had 120 affairs. Tiger and Elin were officially divorced on August 23, 2010.

Career Highlights (through 2009)

97 professional wins
71 PGA Tour wins (3rd all-time)
$94,157,304 in PGA Tour earnings
38 European Tour wins (3rd all-time)
14 Major Championship wins
16 World Golf Championship wins

Major Championships

4 Masters Tournament wins (1997, 2001, 2002, 2005)
3 U.S. Open wins (2000, 2002, 2008)
3 British Open Championships wins (2000, 2005, 2006)
4 PGA Championship wins (1999, 2000, 2006, 2007)

Awards

1st Team–Rolex Junior All-American (1990–93)
Golf World Player of the Year (1993)
Golf World Man of the Year (1994)

Pac-10 Player of the Year (1995)

PGA Tour Rookie of the Year (1996)

Sports Illustrated "Sportsman of the Year" (1996)

PGA Tour Player of the Year (1997, 1999–2003, 2005–07, 2009)

PGA Player of the Year (1997, 1999–2003, 2005–07, 2009)

PGA Tour Money Leader (1997, 1999–2002, 2005–07, 2009)

Vardon Trophy (1999–2003, 2005, 2007, 2009)

Byron Nelson Award (1999–2003, 2005–07, 2009)

FedEx Cup Champion (2007, 2009)

ABC's Wide World of Sports Athlete of the Year (1997, 2000)

Associated Press Male Athlete of the Year (1997, 1999, 2000, 2006)

Associated Press Athlete of the Decade (2009)

ESPN's ESPY Award for Best Male Athlete (1997, 1999–2001)

Mark H. McCormack Award (1998–2009)

Records

Won at least one World Golf Championship (WGC) event every year since they began in 1999

All-time wins leader in World Golf Championships events (50 percent win rate)

All-time money leader in World Golf Championships events

Only player in WGC history to enter the final round outside the lead and come back to win

Won the WGC–World Cup with David Duval in 2000 for a total of 17 World Golf Championship titles

Only player to have held the titles of all three of the pre-2009 events at the same time

Accenture Match Play

Record for most lopsided victory in his first-round match against Stephen Ames in 2006: 9 and 8

Record for the fastest possible win in 18-hole match play

Record for largest margin of victory in the 36-hole final match: 8 and 7 against Stewart Cink in 2008

Tied lowest first 18-hole total: 63

Lowest 36-hole total: 127

Largest 36-hole lead: 5 strokes

Lowest 54-hole total: 194

Largest 54-hole lead: 6 strokes

Lowest 72-hole total: 261

Largest margin of victory: 8 strokes

Only player to record top-10 finishes in each appearance (more than two appearances)

Lowest first 18-hole total: 63 (the course record at The Grove)

Bridgestone Invitational

Lowest 18-hole total: 61

Lowest 36-hole total: 125

Lowest 54-hole total: 192

Lowest 72-hole total: 259

Largest margin of victory: 11 strokes

California Golf Fast Fact

The Golden State is home to 1140 public and private golf courses.

Pebble Beach Golf Links

The Pebble Beach Golf Links in Pebble Beach hugs the coastline on the south side of the Monterey Peninsula. The course opened in 1919 and was designed by Jack Neville and Douglas Grant. It is regarded as one of the most beautiful golf courses in the world and hosted the U.S. Open Championships in 1972, 1982, 1992, 2000 and 2010. The Pebble Beach Company was founded by Samuel Finley Brown Morse—a distant cousin of telegraph inventor Samuel Finley Breese Morse—and is currently owned by Arnold Palmer, Richard Ferris, Peter Ueberroth, Clint Eastwood, William Perocchi and GE Pension.

Tennis

Pancho

The sport of tennis has a rich history that began in Europe several thousand years ago. However, it's a little known fact that Ricardo Alonso González—born in Los Angeles and also known as "Pancho"—was the number one ranked player in the world for a number of years in the 1950s and early 1960s and is considered by many to be the greatest player in the history of the game.

González was introduced to tennis at the age of 12 when his mother gave him a 51-cent racquet. The young Ricardo taught himself how to play the game by watching other players on the public courts in Los Angeles. Tennis soon consumed the majority of his time, and he eventually lost interest in school, which resulted in issues with truant officers and the police.

In general, his adolescence can be described as "rocky." He sometimes even slept over at a tennis shop owned by Frank Poulain that was located near the public courts at Exposition Park.

Even though Pancho was a promising junior, his truancy caused him to be ostracized by the predominantly Anglo-Saxon and upper-class tennis establishment of the 1940s, and he was subsequently banned from playing tournaments. At 15, González was arrested for burglary and sentenced to a year in detention. He then served two years in the Navy just as World War II was ending, receiving a bad-conduct discharge in 1947.

At 19, González was 6-foot-3, weighed 183 pounds and had a height advantage over most players during his era. Even Tony Trabert, who disliked González intensely and was badly beaten by him, was once quoted by the *Los Angeles Times* as saying: "González is the greatest natural athlete tennis has ever known. The way he can move that 6-foot-3-inch frame of his around the court is almost unbelievable. He's just like a big cat...Pancho's reflexes and reactions are God-given talents. He can be moving in one direction, and in the split second it takes him to see that the ball [has been] hit to his weak side, he's able to throw his physical mechanism in reverse and get to the ball in time to reach it with his racquet." Fellow tennis player Gussie Moran said that watching González play was like seeing "a god patrolling his personal heaven."

Pancho was the top player in the world, either amateur or professional, for six consecutive years, from 1955 through 1960. However, many would argue that he was also the best player, or the co-number-one player, in 1952, 1954 and 1961—such a nine-year, world number-one ranking is unequalled. Both Bill Tilden and Rod Laver are considered to have each been the best in the world for seven years. Pancho was the top-ranked American amateur in 1949, and 20 years later, in 1969, he was still the sixth or seventh best player in the world.

In 1968, González was inducted into the International Tennis Hall of Fame in Newport, Rhode Island. And in 1969, at the age of 41 at Wimbledon, González beat Charlie Pasarell to win the longest tennis match ever played up to that point. The five-set match lasted five hours and 12 minutes and was played over a two-day period. The final score was 22–24, 1–6, 16–14, 6–3, 11–9 and was so long that it prompted the advent of tie-break scoring. That match is still remembered as one of the highlights in the history of tennis and has been called one of the "Ten Greatest Matches of the Open Era" by *Tennis* magazine. In 1972, at 44 years of age, Pancho was still playing at a high level and was ranked ninth in the United States. Bobby Riggs once described González as being the greatest player ever over a 20-year period.

González married and divorced six times and had seven children. In March 1995, González was diagnosed with cancer and died four months later. Despite creating a great deal of wealth during his playing career, he died in a similar state of poverty as when he came into the world. In fact, González was so poor at the end of his life that Andre Agassi paid for Pancho's Las Vegas funeral.

Indian Wells Tennis Garden

California is home to the Indian Wells Tennis Garden, a tennis facility that contains the second largest tennis stadium in the world behind Arthur Ashe Stadium in New York. The Indian Wells Tennis Garden is located in Indian Wells in the Coachella Valley, between Palm Desert and La Quinta. The BNP Paribas Open (previously called the Pacific Life Open) is played there, as well as several junior and adult United States Tennis Association (USTA) events throughout the year. The 88-acre facility cost $77 million to build and was opened in March 2000. Stadium court can accommodate 16,100 people, and there are also 11 other match courts, as well as six practice courts and two clay courts.

California Tennis Fast Fact

About 1000 USTA-sanctioned tennis tournaments are held in the state of California each year.

Chapter Seven

Life's a Beach in California

Surfing

Hawaiians Introduce Surfing to California

In 1885, three Hawaiian princes were going to school in San Mateo. They made a trip to Santa Cruz and reportedly rode waves at the mouth of the San Lorenzo River using surfboards that were shaped out of local redwood. In 1907, George Freeth came over from Hawaii and "wowed" Californians with a surfing demonstration at Redondo Beach.

However, famous Hawaiian surfer, Duke Kahanamoku, is credited with introducing the sport to the Golden State. In 1912, Duke passed through Southern California on his way to Sweden to compete as a swimmer in the summer Olympics. His surfing exhibitions caused a great deal of excitement and received much more attention than Freeth's had five years earlier. Thanks to the Hawaiian influence, Californians have been inspired to hit the waves ever since, and the sport is now popular throughout the state.

Hollow is Hotter

Tom Blake was born in Wisconsin but soon made his way out to California. He was a good swimmer and loved spending time at the beach and in the ocean, so it was only logical that he became a lifeguard. In 1924, while working as a lifeguard at the Santa Monica Swimming Club, he paddled out on a surfboard for the first time and was instantly hooked.

However, in 1924, surfboards were still big, awkward, solid pieces of wood and weighed more than 100 pounds. As a result, they were tough to turn and weren't that great in the buoyancy department. Luckily for the sport of surfing, Tom Blake was a visionary, and in 1926, he replicated some old Hawaiian boards and drilled hundreds of holes in the wood, sheathed the board in marine plywood veneer and made some shape modifications. Voila! The world's first hollow surfboard was born! The board was 15 feet long, 19 inches wide, 4 inches thick and weighed much less than the average surfboard of that era.

In 1928, Blake brought his new boards to the first ever Pacific Coast Surfing Championships held in Corona del Mar. He then proceeded to win the paddleboard race by over 100 yards. In 1930, Blake patented his "Hawaiian Hollow Surfboard" and before long, almost all racing paddleboards were hollow.

Surfers were digging them as well because the lighter, more buoyant boards were easier to turn and made surfing even more fun. In addition, the American Red Cross Life Saving Division started using

Blake's boards, and the Hawaiian Hollow Surfboard completely revolutionized the approach to water rescue worldwide.

Blake's boards also had an immediate impact on the sport of surfing and directly resulted in more participation. In 1932, the Thomas N. Rogers Company based in Venice, California, started to manufacture his boards, making it the first production surfboard in the world. Three other manufacturers—Robert Mitchell, the L.A. Ladder Co. and the Catalina Equipment Company—also produced Blake's board all the way up to the early 1950s.

In 1935, Tom Blake was the first person to put a fin on a surfboard to improve directional stability. He also invented the sailing surfboard, the predecessor of today's windsurf board, and the first waterproof camera housing for surf photography.

Blake's innovations inspired other surfers to experiment with all kinds of equipment, and he's credited with being a catalyst for the progression of the sport in the 20th century. He was also the author of several books, and he is the only person besides the legendary Duke Kahanamoku to be inducted into both the Swimming and Surfing Halls of Fame.

Surfboard Engineering

Born in Los Angeles in 1919, Bob Simmons is one of surfing's great innovators. He was involved in an awful bicycle accident as a teenager and was hospitalized with a fractured skull, a broken leg and a shattered elbow. Simmons' body healed up fine except for his elbow, and he took up surfing in 1939 as a way to regain strength and mobility. He studied engineering at Cal Tech in Los Angeles and was an excellent student until World War II started. His arm injury kept him out of the war, so Simmons went to work for Douglas Aircraft instead. During the war, he surfed a lot and didn't have to share many waves as there were few surfers in California while bombs were dropping overseas.

As the war ended, Simmons turned his attention and engineering interest to improving surfboard design. He studied hydrodynamics and began making his own boards, which were much faster than anything being surfed at the time. Simmons quickly became well known at Malibu, a famed surf spot in Southern California, for chasing down slower surfers.

Simmons then began experimenting with new materials such as fiberglass and Styrofoam. And he also played around with several design elements to determine ideal board weight, concaves, aspect ratios, scoops and kicker. Simmons constructed his own molds out of concrete in order to create foam blanks that he could then sculpt to make surfboards.

In 1948, he began covering the entire board with fiberglass, and in the summer of 1949, he reportedly sold over 100 of his revolutionary foam-and-fiberglass boards. This was an impressive feat since it was estimated that there were less than 1000 surfers in the state of California at that time.

Simmons also became interested in weather and wave patterns in an attempt to try to determine where the best waves were in the world. However, all of this innovation and forward thinking was cut short in 1954 when Simmons drowned while surfing in San Diego at the age of 35.

Velzy

Dale Velzy was born in 1927 in Hermosa Beach, and his dad was a lifeguard. When Dale was young, he spent a lot of time at the beach and started skimboarding and bodyboarding. Velzy's dad made him a surfboard when he was eight or nine years old, and it wasn't long before he was hooked.

Velzy eventually began tinkering with surfboard design, and in 1949, he opened the world's first surf shop, called Velzy Surfboards, under the pier at Manhattan Beach. Velzy partnered with another giant in the sport of surfing, Hap Jacobs, and the two are now considered legendary shapers who did a lot to advance surfboard design and surfing's popularity in the early 1950s.

By the mid-1950s, Dale Velzy owned several surf shops in Southern California and Hawaii, but in 1959, the Internal Revenue Service shut down his business for faulty record keeping. However, he kept on shaping and coming up with improved designs right up until the 1990s.

Velzy was open-minded when it came to producing great boards, and he stayed on top of things even as shortboards became more popular in the 1970s. He mentored and inspired countless young surfers and shapers during his lifetime, and a surf spot in Hawaii has been named "Velzyland" in his honor.

Velzy was once quoted as saying, "All I've tried to do is to have fun and do whatever it was as good as I could. Looking back, there's nothing that I'd do different, except that I'd just do more of it. As far as my boards go, I figure they speak for themselves."

Da Bull

Greg "Da Bull" Noll was born in San Diego in 1937. When he was three, his family moved to Manhattan Beach, and that's where, at age 11, he learned to surf. Noll also joined the Manhattan Beach Surf Club and learned how to shape boards from legendary shaper Dale Velzy. In addition, he competed in paddle-boarding as a member of the Los Angeles County Lifeguards and started to develop his big-wave surfing skills at breaks like Lunada Bay in Palos Verdes. Before he finished high school in 1954, he convinced his parents to let him move to the island of O'ahu in Hawaii with a group of older surfers and finish high school there.

His lifeguarding background gave him a lot of confidence to get out and conquer bigger surf. Noll and a group of other Californians first tackled a Hawaiian surf spot known as Makaha and surfed some of the biggest waves they had ever seen. He spent several years lifeguarding in California during the summer, and then headed back to O'ahu each winter in search of massive surf.

Soon, Greg and his buddies headed to the region of the north shore of the island that is now world famous and were some of the first surfers to explore the huge surf in that area. In 1957, he was one of the first to surf

Waimea Bay, Oʻahu. During the 1960s surfing boom, Noll opened up a successful surf shop in Hermosa Beach, California. And in 1969, he rode what was deemed one of the biggest waves in history up to that point at Makaha, even bigger than before.

That ride made him surfing's first big-wave celebrity. His nickname, "Da Bull," was given to him for his stubbornness, but it also fit his powerful and hard-charging surfing style as well as his big stature and personality. Greg was also a renowned surf filmmaker and can be identified in classic footage by his black-and-white-striped shorts.

He closed his Hermosa Beach surf shop in the early 1970s and spent several years commercial fishing in Northern California and Alaska. However, he eventually got back into the surfing scene, shaping boards and organizing surf contests in the Crescent City area where he now lives with his wife.

Invention of the Wetsuit

The Pacific Ocean water temperatures along the California coast can get pretty chilly. In Southern California, average water temps dip into the mid-50°F range in the winter and only get up to around 70°F the summer months. In Central and Northern California, average water temps can get down to around 50°F in the winter and rarely surpass mid-60°F during the summer. As a result, prior to the 1950s, when the first wetsuits came onto the scene, surf sessions in California tended to be relatively short, and few dared to venture out into the water during the winter months.

The invention of the neoprene wetsuit changed all of that, and surfing is now a year-round sport that can be enjoyed for hours at a time regardless of the air and water temperatures. However, there's some difference of opinion when it comes to who should get the credit for this revolutionary contribution to the sport of surfing. There are three Californians that each claim to have invented the neoprene wetsuit independent of one another and around the same time.

In 1951, Hugh Bradner, a professor at the University of California, Berkeley, began developing a suit to keep divers warm in cold water.

In 1952, Jack O'Neill began selling his own wetsuit designs when he opened his first surf shop in San Francisco. O'Neill soon moved the company to Santa Cruz, where O'Neill has become one of the most recognizable surf brands on the planet.

Lastly, in 1953, twin brothers Bob and Bill Meistrell, who founded the popular Body Glove brand, were also reportedly experimenting with neoprene wetsuits.

Jack

What began as a little surf shop in San Francisco in 1952 has now become a multimillion-dollar global empire. However, Jack O'Neill isn't your stereotypical, wealth-creation tycoon—he simply wanted to stay warm.

"I'm just as surprised by this as anyone," O'Neill says. "I was just messing around with rubber."

O'Neill was born in Denver, Colorado, in 1923. He spent his early years in Portland, Oregon, before he and his family eventually moved to Southern California.

He worked as a lumberjack, served in the Army Air Corps and moved to San Francisco in 1949, where he earned a living as a commercial fisherman. He also sold architectural aluminum, fire extinguishers and skylights, but always loved the ocean and would spend his lunch breaks in the frigid water down at Ocean Beach, bodysurfing in swim trunks.

In an effort to stay warm, Jack started stuffing flexible polyvinyl chloride (PVC) into his trunks, but the catalyst for his wetsuit designs came when a scientist friend showed O'Neill a sample of neoprene foam.

In 1952, O'Neill opened his first surf shop—simply called "Surf Shop"—in a garage on San Francisco's Great Highway. He sold balsa boards, wax and the first generation of his neoprene vests. In 1959, Jack headed south in search of warmer weather and better waves and decided to relocate his operation to Santa Cruz.

Right around that time, surfing was becoming very popular along the California coast. Thanks to the Beach Boys, everybody felt like "goin' surfing" in the early '60s, and wetsuits were just what these folks needed. Fortunately, by then O'Neill had figured out how to keep the neoprene from tearing so easily and made wetsuits that were easier to take on and off. The solution he found was to laminate elastic nylon jersey to the surface of the neoprene and to use a zigzag stitch on the seams. In order to keep up with increasing demand, Jack soon opened up a larger manufacturing facility and put his six children to work.

The signature patch Jack wears over his left eye was the result of an accident with a surf leash prototype he was testing out in 1971 at "The Hook," a popular surf spot in Santa Cruz. Pat O'Neill, Jack's son, invented the leash, but the early versions were a little too elastic. Shortly thereafter, the "patch" became the new O'Neill logo and is now recognized around the world.

By 1980, O'Neill Surf Shop had grown into a successful global brand. In 1985, Jack became chairman of the board of O'Neill, Inc., and his son Pat took over as CEO. One of the initiatives Pat O'Neill is responsible for is the establishment of Team O'Neill, which over the decades has included surfing standouts such as Shaun Tomson, Dane Kealoha, Martin Potter, Brad Gerlach, Shane Beschen, Rochelle Ballard, Cory Lopez, Jordy Smith, Timmy Reyes, Bobby Martinez, the Gudauskas brothers and Jon Jon Florence.

Today, O'Neill is the top wetsuit brand in the world, with licensees and distributorships in more than 67 countries.

O'Neill Gives Back

Now that Jack has a little more free time, he supports a school for dyslexic kids, works to save the great white shark from extinction and takes kids for cruises on Monterey Bay on the Team O'Neill catamaran. His Sea Odyssey program educates youth about the microbiology of the Monterey Bay Marine Sanctuary and about our living and endangered oceans.

"As I see it, we've gotten a lot from the ocean, in more ways than one," says O'Neill. "I mean, the ocean has been very comforting to me through the years.

When you get all screwed up, and you jump in the ocean, everything's all right again."

Surf City USA

Huntington Beach is one of California's surfing hotspots. In 2006, the Huntington Beach Conference and Visitors Bureau was awarded the "Surf City USA" trademark. The U.S. Open of Surfing, a weeklong surfing contest, is held there every summer and is part of the Association of Surfing Professionals World Tour qualification process.

The event started in 1959 and was originally named the West Coast Surfing Championship before becoming the United States Surfing Championships in 1964. In 1982, the event became known as the Ocean Pacific Pro, and in 1994, the contest was finally renamed the U.S. Open of Surfing. In addition, Huntington Beach is home to the Surfing Walk of Fame and the Surfers' Hall of Fame.

Big Wave Surfing

Most people equate Hawaii with big-wave surfing. However, is also home to three formidable big-wave surf spots as well, and the best known of them is called Mavericks.

A cold-water wave that breaks a half-mile off Pillar Point in Half Moon Bay, Mavericks gained international attention around 1990 and is now home to the annual Mavericks Surf Contest. There are reports of 100-foot waves seen breaking there in November 2001, but the largest wave that anyone has ever ridden at Mavericks was around 70 feet.

Besides the massive surf and cold water, another hazard at Mavericks is the large boulders inside, also known as "The Boneyard." In 1994, Mark Foo, one of the most highly regarded Hawaiian big-wave surfers, died while surfing this break.

Ghost Trees off the coast of Monterey is another big-wave surf spot. It only breaks a few times a year, but when it does, the waves can be massive. In 2007, big-wave surfer Peter Davi died while surfing Ghost Trees.

The third big-wave spot off the California coast is called Cortes Bank. This break is roughly 100 miles west of San Diego and started to gain gained notoriety in 2001. In 2008, Mike Parsons was photographed riding a 70-foot-plus foot wave there, and it's believed that this spot has the potential to produce a surfable 100-foot wave someday.

16-Year-Old Monster Slayer

On December 19, 1994, a 16-year-old named Jay Moriarty from Santa Cruz paddled out to the break at Mavericks. Many say that the waves that day were some of the biggest ever ridden anywhere in the world up to that time. Moriarty took on one of the monsters, but instead of dropping into the wave, he suffered what has been estimated to be around a 40-foot freefall, leading to one of the most spectacular big-wave wipeouts that has ever been captured on film.

The fall broke his board, and Jay ended up on the cover of *Surfer* magazine for that one—however, it didn't seem to faze him one bit. In fact, once he made it back to the channel after the wipeout, he grabbed another board and paddled right back out to the lineup with a huge smile on his face.

Jay Moriarty became a well-known name in the surfing world from that day forward. However, the fame never got to him. He remained personable, approachable, positive and humble even as he earned a sought-after spot among some of the best big-wave surfers on the planet.

Unfortunately, this incredible surfer's life was cut tragically short. One day before his 23rd birthday, he drowned while free-diving alone in the Maldives.

Mark Foo

On December 23, 1994, a few days after Moriarty became famous at Mavericks, legendary big-wave surfer Mark Foo died there, a devastating blow to the big-wave surfing community at the time. Some believe that Foo was sleep deprived at the time since he had taken an overnight flight from his home in Hawaii to get to California in time to catch the swell.

However, what actually happened after he fell while taking off on a wave estimated to be around 20 feet high (measured from the back of the wave) is a mystery. There are photos of his wipeout from multiple angles that show Foo falling headfirst into the bottom of the wave. One theory is that his leash got caught on a rock, which would have held him down and caused him to drown.

Mike Parsons, another big-wave surfer, later reported coming into contact with something underwater during a fall he took shortly afterward, but no one can be sure whether or not that "something" was actually Foo's body. Two hours after Mark Foo fell, his body turned up inside the Pillar Point lagoon with his ankle still tied to the broken tail section of the board.

Paskowitz Surf Camp

In 1972, Dorian "Doc" Paskowitz founded the Paskowitz Surf Camp. It's now the longest running surf camp in the United States and holds sessions each year on Pacific Beach in San Diego. They advertise that they "don't just teach people to surf—[they] create surfers."

The Paskowitz family—Dorian, his wife Juliette and their nine children—are known as the "First Family of Surfing." Doc was born in 1921 and graduated from Stanford Medical School in Palo Alto in 1946. However, by 1956, he had grown dissatisfied with what his life had become and decided to make a radical change.

He married Juliette shortly thereafter, and the couple chose a nomadic surfing life. They lived out of a 24-foot camper and cruised from surf spot to surf spot, mostly in California. Doc worked as a physician for short stints when they needed money, but they opted not to put down any roots. The Paskowitz clan grew to 11 throughout the 1960s and 1970s, and Doc and Juliette home-schooled, or rather camper-schooled, their nine children.

The entire family surfed religiously, but Israel "Izzy" Paskowitz, the fourth of the nine Paskowitz children, seemed to enjoy their unique lifestyle the most. Izzy spent most of his life surfing, and he and his siblings grew up spending their summers at San Onofre State Beach, in San Diego County, teaching people to surf.

Izzy had a successful professional longboard surfing career, won his first pro event in 1983 and now runs the family surf camp business.

Izzy and his wife, Danielle, have three children, one of which was diagnosed with autism at age three, the inspiration for a nonprofit organization called Surfers Healing, based in San Juan Capistrano, whose mission is to take autistic children surfing.

The Surfrider Foundation

In 1984, a group of surfers in Malibu started the Surfrider Foundation. They originally got together to protect over 30 miles of coastal waters from Marina Del Rey to Ventura County, an area that included their favorite local surf spot at Malibu Point. The organization was an advocacy group to protest various threats to surf spots and water quality until 1991, when the first Surfrider Foundation chapters were founded.

Today, the Surfrider Foundation has chapters around the world, with over 50,000 members, and focuses on water quality, beach access and coastal ecosystem issues. Their mission statement states: "the Surfrider Foundation is a grassroots, nonprofit environmental organization dedicated to the protection and enjoyment of the world's oceans, waves and beaches for all people, through conservation, activism, research and education."

Red Triangle

There are a lot of great surf spots in California; however, some of them are rarely surfed for a variety of reasons: they're difficult to access, are far from any towns or have inconsistent conditions.

Another reason is that some surf spots are considered to be too "sharky"—a term surfers use to describe a break that's popular with sharks, particularly great white sharks. One area of the Northern California coast that is exceptionally sharky has been nicknamed the Red Triangle—the word "red," as you may have guessed, was chosen to describe the color of the water post–shark attack.

The Red Triangle is a triangle-shaped region extending from Bodega Bay (north of San Francisco) to the north, the Farallon Islands to the west and Ano Nuevo (between Santa Cruz and Half Moon Bay) to the south. Some even extend the southern point down to Big Sur because some attacks have occurred in the area between Big Sur and Ano Nuevo. However, sharks are rarely sighted in the vast majority of Monterey Bay, which encompasses a large part of that southern region.

Regardless of where you choose to locate the southern point of the Red Triangle, this region is home to a significant number of elephant seals, harbor seals, sea lions and sea otters, which are all common prey items for the great white shark. Roughly 38 percent of recorded great white shark attacks on humans in the United States and 11 percent of worldwide attacks have happened inside the Red Triangle.

The good news is that shark attacks are still relatively rare, even in the Red Triangle, despite this area of the coast being so popular with surfers and other ocean enthusiasts.

More Wave Riding
Bodyboarding

In 1971, Tom Morey left his surfboard business in California to hang out and work on some new designs in Hawaii. Shortly thereafter, he invented the bodyboard and, by 1977, was producing 80,000 of the boards per year. A couple of years later, in 1979, the first professional bodyboarding contest was held in Huntington Beach. The event was called the Morey/Gap and was won by a Californian named Mike Lambresi. Lambresi later switched to conventional surfing and became a three-time U.S. professional champion.

Fast Fact

On October 22, 2010, Lucas Ransom, a 19-year-old bodyboarder, was killed by a great white shark on Surf Beach in Santa Barbara County. The shark is estimated to have been between 15 and 20 feet long. It was the 12th confirmed fatal shark attack in California waters since 1950.

Bodysurfing

California is home to one of the most famous bodysurfing spots in the world, "the Wedge" in Newport Beach. On big swells, wave faces at the Wedge can be over 30 feet tall, and this spot attracts some of the best bodysurfers in the sport.

In 1964, the Gillis Beach Bodysurfing Association (GBBA) was formed and is now the oldest bodysurfing club in the United States. The club started on the beaches of Playa Del Rey in Los Angeles. The first-ever bodysurfing contest was held at Pipeline on the north shore of O'ahu in 1971. In fact, that first bodysurfing event took place several months before the first conventional surfing event was ever held at that world-famous break.

In 1977, the first World Bodysurfing Championships was held in Oceanside, and the annual contest remains the biggest bodysurfing competition in the world besides the annual competition at Pipeline. The GBBA have also been holding another longtime bodysurfing contest at Manhattan Beach. The Manhattan Beach Bodysurfing Contest is a part of the annual International Surf Festival held at Manhattan Beach and is usually held in August.

Skimboarding

In the late 1920s, lifeguards in Laguna Beach started what has now become the sport of skimboarding. For years, all skimboards were made of wood, but today, top professionals are using boards that are more high-tech than the average surfboard. Skimboarding has gained a lot of popularity worldwide in recent years, though Laguna Beach is still considered by many to be the epicenter of the sport because most of the top professional skimboarders have come from that area.

In the early 1960s, one Laguna Beach rider named Mike Buxton started performing aerials while skimboarding. And in the mid-1970s, Tex Haines and Peter Prietto started Victoria Skimboards, named after a popular skimboard beach. Their company became not only a popular board manufacturer, but in the late 1970s, also started to organize the first skimboarding contests.

In the late 1980s, a Laguna Beach local named Tom Trager landed on the cover of *Sports Illustrated*. However, the caption said that Tom was surfing when he was actually skimboarding. In the late '80s and early '90s the sport experienced a lull, but since the mid-1990s, the sport's popularity has been steadily growing.

Stand-up Paddle Surfing

Stand-up paddle (SUP) surfing is an ancient form of surfing that originated in Hawaii. Rick Thomas, a Navy special forces Vietnam veteran, is credited with being the first surfer to introduce California to stand-up paddle surfing. In 2000, Thomas began SUP surfing in San Diego, and it's now one of the fastest growing sports in the state of California. And since SUP's California debut, the sport is also gaining immense popularity on lakes, rivers and in coastal communities around the world.

One place in particular that stand-up paddling has become popular is Lake Tahoe. Tahoe is the largest alpine lake in North America, located on the California–Nevada border. In 2007, Ernie Brassard, Bob Pearson and Rick Thomas started a race on Lake Tahoe called the "Ta-Hoe Nalu." That first summer, the event had 34 participants. By 2010, the event had grown into a full-blown Ta-Hoe Nalu Paddle Festival and held six races over a two-day period for several hundred paddlers.

Kitesurfing

Kitesurfing is very popular in some parts of California, including Coronado, Long Beach, Lake Isabella,

Ventura County, Pismo Beach, north of Santa Cruz and the San Francisco Bay Area. It's an exciting sport, but unfortunately, there have been several tragic kitesurfing accidents over the years. One such accident occurred in July 2010 in San Simeon to Kinsley Thomas Wong, widely regarded as the father of kitesurfing on the Central Coast of California.

Wong is the founder of XtremeBigAir, a kitesurfing shop that he started in Pismo Beach in 1994. The 43-year-old Wong is known for his aerial maneuvers and huge smile. In 1999, his business became the first IKO (International Kiteboarding Organization) certified kiteboarding school in the nation with an Advanced Kiteboarding Instructor rating.

In July 2010, Wong, an expert kiteboarder, was carried out of the water and smashed onto some rocks by a large gust of wind. He was quickly airlifted to a nearby hospital but suffered serious head and neck injuries. His accident drew a lot of attention in the kitesurfing community and served as a reminder to both novice and expert enthusiasts that harnessing the wind can be unpredictable at times. Kinsley Thomas Wong was not wearing a helmet at the time of the accident.

Chapter Eight

CA = Action Sports Mecca

X Games

The Next Gen Olympics

Xtreme dude! The word "extreme" has been used heavily over the past 20 years to describe various aspects of high-action sports. And, to many of us, what these athletes do is extreme because we have a tough time imagining ourselves ever attempting to do some of the tricks and stunts that they pull off with such practiced ease. However, just like in any other sport, athletes in BMX, skateboarding and motocross expand their comfort zones over time. For many of them, what they do is not extreme at all, so now the word "action" is more commonly used.

ESPN's X Games have become synonymous with action sports, and they have become the Olympics for a lot of the sports that are represented. At the X Games, the best of the best in the world come to compete for medals. However, make no mistake, unlike the Olympics, this is an invitation-only, highly commercial, annual sports event that is controlled by ESPN, which is also why it's so entertaining and is covered so well!

The various events for the very first X Games were held in the summer of 1995 in Rhode Island and Vermont, and in 1996, all of the events were held in Rhode Island. In 1997, ESPN launched the first Winter X Games in Big Bear, California, featuring winter action-sports athletes. The Winter X Games are usually held in January each year, and the Summer X Games have been held in California each summer since 1997 with the exception of 2001 and 2002, when they were held in Pennsylvania.

Athletes compete for gold, silver and bronze medals, as well as prize money, and many participants wait for the X Games to unveil the new tricks that they've been perfecting.

California Summer X Games Highlights

X Games Three: San Diego, June 1997
- 221,200 spectators

X Games Four: San Diego, June 1998
- 233,000 spectators

X Games Five: San Francisco, June/July 1999
- 275,000 spectators
- It was the first professional sporting event to be fully broadcast live on the Internet.
- Tony Hawk (professional skateboarder) landed a 900-degree spin.
- Travis Pastrana (professional motocross rider) scored a record high 99.00-point run to win the first-ever Moto-X Freestyle event.

X Games Six: San Francisco, August 2000
- Dave Mirra (professional BMX rider) landed the first-ever double backflip in competition to win the BMX Park event.
- Tommy Clowers (professional motocross rider) won the first-ever Moto-X Step Up event; he hit a record-breaking height of 35 feet.
- Bucky Lasek (professional skateboarder) got the highest score in X Games history (98.50) in the Skateboard Vert event.

X Games Nine: Los Angeles, August 2003
- Brian Deegan (professional motocross rider) landed the first-ever 360 in Freestyle Moto-X and captured the gold medal in the Big Air/Best Trick event.
- Ryan Sheckler (professional skateboarder) won gold in the Skateboard Streetpark event, becoming the youngest X Games gold medalist ever at the age of 13.

X Games Ten: Long Beach and Los Angeles, August 2004
- Nate Adams (professional motocross rider) became the first rider to defeat Travis Pastrana at the X Games in the Freestyle Moto-X event.
- Danny Way (professional skateboarder) won the first Skateboard Big Air event.
- Jeremy McGrath (professional motocross rider) won gold in Moto-X and bronze in Supermoto at his first X Games.
- Chuck Carothers (professional motocross rider) got gold in the Moto-X Best Trick event with the X Games' first body varial, a skateboarding trick

that involves turning in midair without the feet being in contact with the board.

X Games Eleven: Los Angeles, August 2005
- ESPN removed inline skating from the Summer X Games.
- Shaun White (professional skateboarder and snowboarder) attempted to land a 1080 spin 29 times but was unable to get it done.
- Jamie Bestwick (professional BMX rider) nailed the first double tailwhip flair in the BMX Vert Best Trick event.
- Travis Pastrana (professional motocross rider) won the gold medal in Moto-X Freestyle and became the athlete with most medals in Moto-X.
- ESPN agreed to keep the X Games in Los Angeles through 2009.

X Games Twelve: Long Beach and Los Angeles, August 2006
- Travis Pastrana (professional motocross rider) executed the world's first double backflip on a dirt bike; he also won gold in the Moto X Best Trick event with a record high score of 98.60.
- Kevin Robinson (professional BMX rider) landed the double flair for the first time.
- Travis Pastrana (professional motocross rider and rally car driver) won the gold medal in the first X Games Rally event.
- Chad Kagy (professional BMX rider) nailed the first flatwhip double tailwhip 540.

X Games Thirteen: Long Beach and Los Angeles, August 2007
- Jake Brown (professional skateboarder) landed the first 720 in Big Air competition and, on his next trick, took the worst spill in X Games skateboard history.
- Ricky Carmichael (professional motocross rider) won the gold medal in the first Moto-X Racing Circuit event.
- Simon Tabron (professional BMX rider) pulled off back-to-back 900s in the BMX Vert event, an X Games first.
- Shaun White (professional skateboarder and snowboarder) won the gold medal in the Skateboard Vert event.

X Games Fourteen: Los Angeles, July/August 2008
- Danny Way (professional skateboarder) caught his shins on the lip of the quarterpipe after a 20-plus-foot fall during the Big Air event, recording the second worst crash at the X Games behind Jake Brown's in 2007.
- Ryan Sheckler (professional skateboarder) won his second gold at the X Games with a win in the Street Skateboarding event.
- Kyle Loza (professional motocross rider) unveiled a new move called "The Electric Doom" to win gold in the Moto-X Best Trick event, his second X Games gold.
- Andy Macdonald (professional skateboarder) won his 15th medal at the X Games, replacing Tony Hawk as the all-time leader in skateboarding medals.

- Travis Pastrana (professional motocross rider and rally car driver) won gold in the Rally X event.
- Jim DeChamp (professional motocross rider) attempted the first front flip on a motocross bike but was unable to land it.
- Tarah Gieger (professional motocross rider) won the gold in the X Games' first women's supercross event.
- Jeremy Lusk (professional motocross rider) won a gold medal in the Freestyle Moto-X competition.

X Games Fifteen: Los Angeles, July/August 2009
- Jake Brown (professional skateboarder) won his first gold medal in the Big Air Skateboarding event.
- Danny Way (professional skateboarder) won gold in the first Big Air Rail Jam event at the X Games, a competition that he helped create.
- Paul Rodriguez (professional skateboarder) won gold in the Skateboard Street event.
- Kyle Loza (professional motocross rider) won the gold medal in the Moto-X Best Trick event by doing the same move he won with in 2008 ("The Electric Doom"), despite the judges stating before the event that innovation would win the gold; he also became the first rider to three-peat in that event.
- Ricky Carmichael (professional motocross rider) and Ronnie Renner (professional motocross rider) both won gold medals in the Moto-X Step Up event after Carmichael took a nasty fall.
- Anthony Napolitan (professional BMX rider) pulled off the first double front flip on a bicycle.

- Travis Pastrana (professional motocross rider) attempted a rodeo 720 (aka "The Toilet Paper Roll") in the Moto-X Best Trick event but was unable to land it.
- Blake Williams (professional motocross rider from Australia) won the gold medal in the Freestyle Moto-X event and became the first non-American rider to do so.
- Jamie Bestwick (professional BMX rider) won gold in the BMX Vert event, three-peating in the event.
- Pierre-Luc Gagnon (professional skateboarder) won the gold medal in the Skate Vert event for the second year in a row.
- Ashley Fiolek (professional motocross rider) won the gold medal in the women's Moto-X Super X event at the age of 18 and also became the first X Games deaf medalist.

X Games Sixteen: Los Angeles, July/August 2010
- Travis Pastrana (professional motocross rider) won the gold medal in the Freestyle Moto-X event by landing the first double backflip at the X Games in that competition and also won his first gold medal in the Moto-X Speed and Style event.
- Ashley Fiolek (professional motocross rider) won the gold medal in the women's Moto-X Super X event for the second consecutive year and became the first rider to accomplish that feat.
- Matt Buyten (professional motocross rider) won the gold medal in the Moto X Step Up event.
- Jamie Bestwick (professional BMX rider) won the gold medal in the BMX Vert event and became the first rider to four-peat.

- Pierre-Luc Gagnon (professional skateboarder) won the gold medal in the Skateboard Vert event and became the first skateboarder to three-peat in that event.
- Garrett Reynolds (professional BMX rider) won the gold medal in the BMX Street event and became the first athlete to three-peat in that event.
- Cam Sinclair (professional motocross rider) won the gold medal in the Moto-X Best Trick event with a double backflip, just one year after a horrific crash nearly ended his life.
- Ryan Sheckler (professional skateboarder) won the gold medal in the Skateboarding Street event.

Skateboarding

Sidewalk Surfers

Surfers in California in the late 1940s and early 1950s are believed to have been the first skateboarders. When the waves were flat, several surfers started experimenting with ways to have fun cruising the streets and sidewalks on boards or boxes fitted with roller-skate wheels. This early activity was called "Sidewalk Surfing," and surfers rode around on these boards, emulating the surfing maneuvers and style of that era.

Although it's unclear exactly where in California this early version of skateboarding first popped up, the new pastime spread throughout the state relatively quickly, and it wasn't long before people were using pressed layers of wood for the deck and figuring out ways to make them more maneuverable.

In 1956, the first manufactured skateboard decks were ordered by surf shop owner Bill Richard in Los Angeles, and the Chicago Roller Skate Company produced sets of wheels that could be attached to the bottom. These first decks were simple planks of wood painted with various designs.

By the 1960s, numerous surfboard manufacturers began jumping on the skateboarding phenomenon and started producing decks that were designed like mini surfboards. Soon, surfing companies such as Jack's, Hobie and Makaha were sponsoring skateboarding contests and were assembling teams to promote the products.

The sport quickly became popular enough to inspire the creation of a national magazine dedicated to it: *Skateboarder Magazine*. And in 1965, the international championships for skateboarding were even broadcast on national television.

However, around 1966, skateboard sales slowed down dramatically, and *Skateboarder Magazine* closed down its operation. Although several companies were manufacturing complete skateboard decks that had roller skate–type wheels included by the late 1960s, the overall popularity of the sport was relatively low for the remainder of that decade.

The lull in skateboarding ended in the early 1970s, thanks in large part to new skateboard innovations such as the development of the pure polyurethane wheel. This new wheel improved skateboard traction in a big way, and skateboard performance reached an entirely new level.

Another boost to the resurgence of the sport was the development of skate trucks that made the boards more maneuverable and allowed skaters to try more advanced tricks. These advancements in skateboard design were the catalyst for a whole new generation of skaters to push the envelope and, in turn, ignite what has become the immense global popularity of skateboarding today.

Z-Boys

In the 1970s, the Z-Boys, a group of skateboarders from Santa Monica and Venice revolutionized the sport. These skateboarders were the catalyst for modern skateboarding and the skater subculture. The Z-Boys got their name from the Zephyr Competition Skate Team, which was sponsored by the Jeff Ho Surfboards and Zephyr Productions surf shop in the Venice Beach area of Santa Monica.

The Z-Boys were some of the first skaters to drop into empty Southern California swimming pools during the 1976 drought. The vertical walls of the pools inspired them to experiment with aerial and sliding moves that became the basis for the aerial style of skateboarding that is so popular today. As a result, many consider the Z-Boys to be the most influential skateboarding group in the history of the sport.

The Z-Boys have been the subject of numerous books and films, including *Dogtown and Z-Boys*, a movie that won the best documentary honors at the Sundance Film Festival.

Original Z-Boy Members

- Jay Adams
- Tony Alva
- Bob Biniak
- Chris Cahill
- Paul Constantineau
- Shogo Kubo
- Jim Muir
- Peggy Oki (only female member)
- Stacy Peralta
- Nathan Pratt
- Wentzle Ruml
- Allen Sarlo

The Fall

Professional skateboarder Jake "Ironman" Brown was born in Sydney, Australia, in 1974. Jake started to compete in 1996 and turned pro in 1997. On August 2, 2007, at the Summer X Games in Los Angeles, Brown experienced a death-defying fall in the Big Air Skateboarding event. The ESPN commentators called it the "heaviest slam we have ever seen."

During his fifth and final run, Brown landed the first 720 on a mega ramp in competition. However, on his next trick, he lost his balance and flew into the air. Brown fell roughly 45 feet before crashing onto the ramp.

According to Brown, he was too far to the left as he approached the quarterpipe, but the board began to slide when he started to bring it back to the right. When Brown reached the peak of the ramp, he lost foot contact with the board and started to flail boardless in the air. Jake landed on his back on the flat part of the ramp, and the force of the fall knocked his shoes right off.

He lay there, unconscious and motionless, for eight minutes after the vicious crash. However, amazingly, he was able to walk away from the scene, albeit with some assistance. Brown spent three days in the hospital and suffered a fractured wrist, bruised lung and liver, whiplash, ruptured spleen and concussion. The crash has been uploaded to YouTube several times and has been viewed millions of times.

Tony Hawk

Anthony Hawk was born in San Diego in 1968 and is the most recognizable professional skateboarder in the world. He has had an extremely successful career and is considered by many to be one of the most influential pioneers of vertical skateboarding in the modern era.

Tony started skateboarding when he was eight years old. His dad built a ramp in the backyard for him and his brother to practice on, and at age 14, Hawk turned pro. He was a dominating force at the X Games from 1995 to 2002, has been featured in several video games and has had a very active film and television career—Hawk has appeared in movies such as *Police Academy 4: Citizens on Patrol, Gleaming the Cube, Deck Dogz, The New Guy* and *Jackass: The Movie*.

Hawk's Medal Count

X Games Totals: nine gold, three silver, two bronze
  1995: Gold, Vert
  1995: Silver, Park

1996: Silver, Vert
1997: Gold, Vert
1997: Gold, Vert Doubles
1998: Gold, Vert Doubles
1998: Bronze, Vert
1999: Gold, Vert Doubles
1999: Gold, Vert Best Trick
1999: Bronze, Vert
2000: Gold, Vert Doubles
2001: Silver, Vert Best Trick
2001: Gold, Vert Doubles
2002: Gold, Vert Doubles

Landing a 900

On July 27, 1999, Tony Hawk became the first skater to land a "900" in competition, at the Summer X Games in San Francisco, California. It took him 12 attempts to successfully execute the two-and-a-half rotation trick. Then, in 2001 and 2009, he nailed the 900 two more times—at the 2001 Summer X Games in Philadelphia and at a demo in Beverly Hills for the 2009 Tony Hawk: RIDE Presents Stand Up for Skateparks.

Motocross, Supercross and BMX

Battle Anaheim

Many motocross and Supercross fans consider the race that took place at Anaheim Stadium on January 18, 1986, to be the greatest event in American Supercross history. Over 71,000 fans turned out that night and witnessed an epic battle between David Bailey and Rick Johnson.

The two Honda riders passed each other several times for almost 20 laps and both were giving it all they had. Bailey ended up winning that race, but Johnson went on to win the American Motorcyclist Association Supercross national championship later that year. Unfortunately, the rivalry between the two ended when David Bailey was paralyzed in a crash during practice shortly before the start of the 1987 season.

Rick Johnson

Born in 1964 in El Cajon, Rick Johnson is one of the most successful motocross and Supercross racers ever. He was a force to be reckoned with in the 1980s and won seven American Motorcyclist Association national championships from 1984 to 1988—the AMA Motocross (250cc) in 1984, 1986 and 1987; the AMA Motocross (500cc) in 1987 and 1988; and the AMA Supercross in 1986 and 1988.

Johnson started riding at the age of three and turned pro at 16. In 1984, he won his first national championship with the Yamaha factory motocross team. In 1986, he switched to Honda and became the 250cc national champ as well as the top Supercross rider. That season, Johnson and David Bailey, who was also with Honda, battled it out in one of the most intense races in Supercross history at Anaheim Stadium in Anaheim.

Rick Johnson was on fire in 1987 and won the AMA Motocross 250cc and 500cc titles. That same year, he also won the Super Bowl of Motocross at the Los Angeles Memorial Coliseum in dramatic fashion. Johnson crashed in the first corner but charged hard from the back to pass Jeff Ward and Guy Cooper for the win.

Johnson also had a strong season in 1988, winning both the AMA Motocross 500cc and the AMA Supercross title. He retired in 1991 and, in 1999, was inducted into the AMA Motorcycle Hall of Fame.

The Comeback

Cam Sinclair is a professional motocross rider from Australia who won the gold medal in the Moto-X Best Trick event at X Games Sixteen in Los Angeles during the summer of 2010. What made the win so impressive is that he won it by sticking a double backflip, the same trick that nearly cost him his life a year earlier at the Red Bull X-Fighters competition in Madrid, Spain.

In that event, Cam sustained massive injuries after under-rotating while attempting a double backflip and slamming down hard into the ramp. The crash left Sinclair unconscious and in critical condition. He broke his shoulder and cheekbone, ruptured his liver and suffered brain bruising. He was in an induced coma for a week and underwent emergency surgery to stop internal bleeding as well as surgery for his broken shoulder.

Through intensive therapy, Cam was able to walk and eventually ride again. Many regard his comeback in Los Angeles a year later as the greatest in action-sports history.

Motocross Fast Fact

In 1968, four years before the start of the AMA National Motocross Championship, a world-class motocross track was built at an elevation of 8000 feet in the Sierra Nevadas of California. Shortly thereafter, Dave McCoy of the Mammoth Mountain Ski Area got involved and the Mammoth Motocross was born. It's now the oldest and longest running motocross race in the United States.

BMX

California is credited as being the birthplace of bicycle motocross, more commonly known as BMX. The motorcycle-racing documentary, *On Any Sunday*, which was released in 1972, had an opening scene that showed kids riding their bikes on dirt. Soon, all the kids in Southern California were racing their bikes on dirt tracks as a way of emulating the sport of motocross.

By the mid-1970s, BMX racing was popular in several areas of California and was beginning to gain momentum nationally. In response to the popularity of the new sport, manufacturers began creating BMX bikes in the mid-1970s as well.

Today, the sport is one of the main events at the annual Summer X Games. And in 2003, the International Olympic Committee made BMX a full medal Olympic sport for the 2008 Summer Olympics in Beijing.

Chapter Nine

Endurable Californians

Triathlon

Origins

The earliest tri-sport event is believed to have taken place in France in 1902 and involved running, cycling and canoeing. A few other tri-sport events with various formats were held in France from the 1920s to 1960s. However, the first modern tri-sport event involving swimming, cycling and running took place in San Diego on September 25, 1974. It was the first race to actually be called a "triathlon" and was organized by Jack Johnstone and Don Shanahan. The event drew 46 participants and was sponsored by the San Diego Track Club.

Tri Training Tragedy

Great white sharks have attacked several swimmers off the California coast, but fortunately, fatal attacks are rare despite the large increase in the number of ocean swimmers over the past several decades. The most recent fatal attack occurred on April 25, 2008, at Solana Beach, located in the northern part of San Diego County. A group of nine swimmers from the Triathlon Club of San Diego were swimming roughly 150 yards from the beach and one of them, Dr. David Martin—a retired veterinarian and triathlete—was attacked and killed by a large great white shark around 7:00 AM.

Dr. Martin was apparently swimming near the rear of the group when he was suddenly and violently pulled below the surface. He reappeared at the surface and yelled out to his fellow swimmers for help, but by then a large area of water around him was already red. The other swimmers helped him back to shore, where local Del Mar lifeguards tried to save Martin's life, but he died before 8:00 AM of shock and heart failure from massive wounds on both thighs and significant blood loss.

Dr. Richard Rosenblatt, a shark expert, examined the width of the bite area and estimated that the 22-inch mark left by the great white shark that attacked Dr. Martin was consistent with that of a 12- to 15-foot shark.

Cycling

Greg LeMond

Born in 1961 in Lakewood, Greg LeMond was the first non-European bicycle racer to win the Tour de France—in fact, he won it three times: in 1986, 1989 and 1990. In 1978, at the age of 17, LeMond wrote out a list of goals: to win the 1979 Junior World Championship Road Race, to win the 1980 Olympics

Road Race, to win a professional World Championship by the age of 22 and to earn a Tour de France victory by the time he turned 25.

Amazingly, he achieved almost all of those lofty goals pretty much exactly as he had envisioned them. He won the 1979 Junior Championship, then made the 1980 U.S. Olympic Cycling Team. However, President Carter's decision to boycott the 1980 Olympics in Moscow to protest the Soviet invasion of Afghanistan prevented him from having a chance to win the road race there. At the age of 22, he won the World Championships, and in 1986, at the age of 25, he won his first Tour de France.

However, LeMond was unable to defend his title and take home another yellow jersey in 1987 or 1988 because he was shot while turkey hunting about 20 miles northeast of Sacramento. On April 20, 1987, his brother-in-law, Patrick Blades, was firing at a turkey in heavy brush. LeMond, who was on the other side of the brush, was hit in the back by dozens of shotgun pellets.

He made enough of a recovery to compete in the 1989 Tour de France, but he was reportedly racing with 37 shotgun pellets still in his body, two of which were lodged in the lining of his heart. LeMond was 50 seconds behind the leader, Laurent Fignon, going into the final stage, which was an individual time trial that finished in Paris. LeMond beat Fignon by 58 seconds in that stage and won the Tour de France by a mere eight seconds, the closest margin in the event's history.

That same year, LeMond won the world road championship as well and was named *Sports Illustrated*'s 1989 Sportsman of the Year, becoming the first cyclist to receive the award. He went on to win the Tour for the third time in 1990, retired from racing in 1994 and was inducted into the United States Bicycling Hall of Fame in 1996.

Cycling Fast Fact

There has been a nationwide reduction in serious injuries and deaths in the past 10 years, but there were still 109 bicyclists killed on California roads in 2007, and the Golden State routinely has one of the highest cycling fatality rates in the country.

Tour of California

The Amgen Tour of California began in 2006 and has become a highly regarded professional cycling event. The Tour features over 100 pros from all around the world racing for more than 700 miles from northern to Southern California.

The 2008 race attracted 1.8 million spectators and set a record for a single sporting event in the state of California, as well as for any cycling event ever held in the United States. In addition, it's been estimated that the 2008 event was responsible for at least $100 million in economic growth for the state. Professional cyclist Levi Leipheimer, who lives in Santa Rosa, has won the Overall for the Tour of California in three of the five years it's been held thus far (2007, 2008, 2009).

Get Off the Dope

The U.S. cycling team had some incredible success at the 1984 Summer Olympic Games in Los Angeles. They won a total of nine medals out of a possible 24, far more than any other nation, and they snatched gold in four of the eight events.

Steve Hegg from Dana Point won a gold medal in the individual pursuit and shared silver with David Grylls, Patrick McDonough and Leonard Nitz for the team pursuit. Alexi Grewal and Connie Carpenter each took home a gold in the men's and women's individual road races with Rebecca Twig earning a silver. Mark Gorski grabbed gold in the individual sprint and Nelson Vails took home the silver. Leonard Nitz won a bronze in the individual pursuit and Ron Kiefel, Clarence Knickman, Davis Phinney and Andrew Weaver all earned bronze medals for the men's team time trial.

However, all that success was tainted when the world found out that the riders had received blood transfusions, also known as "blood-doping," before their events. Transfusions increase red blood cell counts so that more oxygen can get to an athlete's working muscles. The national team coach at the time was Eddie Borysewicz.

Eddie apparently created a clinic in his hotel room to do the deed, and four of the U.S. athletes who won medals—Hegg, McDonough, Nitz and Twigg—all admitted to getting the transfusions. Luckily for the athletes, they all got to keep their medals since the United States Cycling Federation didn't ban blood-doping until 1985 and the International Olympic Committee didn't ban it until 1986.

Mountain Biking
How Did It All Start?

In 1896, an African American United States Army Cavalry Regiment known as the Buffalo Soldiers modified bicycles to be used in an off-road expedition from Missoula, Montana, to Yellowstone Park and back. However, the sport of mountain biking didn't really begin until the 1970s, and many regard California as its birthplace.

In 1974, a group known as the Cupertino Riders came to a cyclocross race in Marin County with what many consider to be the first true mountain bikes. Also in the mid-1970s, riders in Marin County were modifying heavy "cruiser" bikes with higher quality brakes and wide tires to bomb down mountain trails in the area—they called them "klunkers."

These early versions of the modern mountain bike were built on frames such as the ones Schwinn produced for their Excelsior cruiser bicycle, with gears and BMX-style handlebars added. The first races were held on Mount Tamalpais in Marin County, and from 1976 to 1984, other downhill, off-road races also sprang up in Fairfax.

In the late 1970s and early 1980s, small bicycle manufacturers began making mountain bikes that were more high-tech and lightweight. In 1978, a fellow by the name of Joe Breeze from Mill Valley introduced what many describe as the first mountain bike.

In 1979, Tom Ritchey, Gary Fisher and Charlie Kelly teamed up to create a company they called MountainBikes and started building frames for fat-tire bikes, becoming the first business to exclusively sell mountain bikes. In 1983, the partners parted ways—MountainBikes became known as Fisher Mountain Bikes, and Tom Ritchey started his own frame shop.

Big players in the bicycle industry such as Schwinn and Fuji weren't quick to jump on the mountain bike phenomenon. However, in 1981, Specialized, a company that started in 1974 in Morgan Hill, started to mass-produce mountain bike frames in factories in Japan and Taiwan. That same year, the first major production mountain bike, the Specialized Stumpjumper, came onto the scene.

Swimming

It Must Be the Water...

There must be something about California water, or maybe it's the chlorine content of California pools, that helps develop world-class swimmers. Buster Crabbe, Mark Spitz, Shirley Babashoff, Matt Biondi, Amanda Beard and Natalie Coughlin (just to name a few) were all born in the Golden State.

Flash Gordon

Clarence Linden Crabbe II, also known as "Buster," was born in Oakland in 1908. He went to college at the University of Southern California and, in 1931, was their first All-American swimmer. Buster also won a gold medal in the 400-meter freestyle at the 1932 Olympic Games in Los Angeles and a bronze in the 1500-meter freestyle at the 1928 Olympics in Amsterdam.

After swimming, Crabbe enjoyed a successful film and television career from 1933 to 1979. He starred in over 100 movies and played characters such as Tarzan, Flash Gordon and Buck Rogers.

Mark the Shark

Mark Spitz, also known as "Mark the Shark," was born in Modesto in 1950. His family moved to Hawaii when he was two but then moved to Sacramento when he was six. When Spitz was 14, the family then moved to Santa Clara so he could train with the Santa Clara Swim Club. He attended Santa Clara High School from 1964 to 1968.

By the time the 1968 Olympic Games in Mexico City rolled around, Mark Spitz had already broken 10 world records and was a medal favorite for several events. He took home two gold medals, a silver and a bronze in his Olympic debut, but he was disappointed with his performance.

Spitz went to Indiana University from 1968 to 1972 and won eight individual NCAA titles while he was there. He then proceeded to light the 1972 Olympic pool on fire by winning seven gold medals and setting seven new world records in each event, before retiring at the age of 22. Mark the Shark's record of seven gold medals in a single Olympic Games stood until 2008, when Michael Phelps rocked the swimming world in Beijing.

Surly Shirley

Shirley Babashoff was born in Whittier in 1957. One of the nicknames she was given was "Surly Shirley," and she set six world records and won eight Olympic medals—one gold and two silver at the 1972 Olympics, and one gold and four silver at the 1976 Olympic Games. That's a pretty impressive career; however, it's clear now that she was robbed of accomplishing even more.

At the age of 19, Babashoff was one of the best swimmers in the world when she showed up in Montreal for the 1976 Olympics. She competed in all four of the freestyle races as well as both relays, and many believe Babashoff should have walked away with at least five gold medals at those Games. Instead, she only took home one. Babashoff finished second four times to an East German in Montreal.

In fact, the East German women's swimming team won all but two gold medals in 1976. Shirley also finished second to an East German 10 more times at the 1972 Olympics and at the 1973 and 1975 World Championships. Pure dominance? Not exactly—the East German swimmers were later discovered to have been cheating by using performance-enhancing drugs.

In essence, Babashoff was a victim of the systematic East German steroid campaign, and unfortunately, the International Olympic Committee has never gone back to right those wrongs. To make matters worse, in the summer of 1976, Babashoff was seen as a sore loser when she made accusations that the East German swimmers were cheating.

Babashoff went on to coach swimming before eventually taking a job delivering mail for a post office in Orange County. In a 2004 interview, she was quoted as saying, "They [the East German swimmers] had gotten so big, and when we heard their voices, we thought we were in a coed locker room. I don't know why it wasn't obvious to other people, too. I guess I was the scapegoat."

Swimming Fast Fact

According to USA Swimming's 2009 Membership Report, over 15 percent of the organization's year-round athletes live in one state: California.

Bionic Biondi

Matt Biondi was born in Palo Alto in 1965, went to high school in Moraga and attended the University of California, Berkeley. He swam and played water polo at Berkeley and, in 1984, qualified for a spot on the U.S. Olympic 4 x 100 meter freestyle relay team. Biondi helped the team win a gold medal at the 1984 Olympic Games in Los Angeles.

Biondi then went on to win seven more medals (five gold, one silver and one bronze) in the 1988 Olympics in Seoul and three more (two gold and one silver) at the 1992 Olympics in Barcelona. He has been inducted into both the United States Olympic Hall of Fame and the International Swimming Hall of Fame. He now teaches math in Hawaii, where he lives with his wife and children.

Newport Beach Mermaid

Amanda Beard was born in Newport Beach in 1981 and went to high school in Irvine. At just 14 years of age, she made her Olympic debut at the 1996 Olympic Games in Atlanta, where she won one gold and two silver medals and became the second-youngest Olympic medalist in American swimming history.

In 2000, Amanda captured a bronze at the Olympic Games in Sydney, and she took home three more medals (one gold and two silver) from the 2004 Olympics in Athens. She also competed at the 2008 Olympics but has since focused her efforts on a career as a model, spokeswoman and sports correspondent.

Eleven and Counting...

Natalie Coughlin was born in Vallejo in 1982. She went to high school in Concord before attending the University of California, Berkeley. Coughlin has already won 11 Olympic medals at two Olympic Games. In 2004, she won two gold medals, two silver and one bronze. And in 2008, Natalie won one gold, two silver and three bronze medals in Beijing. If she can grab two more medals at the 2012 Olympics in London, she'll become the most decorated female U.S. Olympian in history.

Running

Big Sur Marathon

The Big Sur International Marathon was established in 1986 and is a point-to-point race from Big Sur to Carmel. The course is on Highway One, the nation's first nationally designated Scenic Highway, and follows the California coastline. Many runners regard the Big Sur International Marathon as the most beautiful marathon on the planet, and it's the top-rated marathon in *The Ultimate Guide to Marathons*.

Big Sur Course Records
Male: 1987, Brad Hawthorne, 2:16:39
Female: 1996, Svetlana Vasilyeva, 2:41:34

Western States 100 – Ultramarathon

The Western States Endurance Run, also known as the Western States 100, is an annual 100-mile-long ultramarathon race in California that officially began in 1977. The event begins at the Squaw Valley ski resort in the Sierra Nevadas and ends in Auburn. The course climbs 18,000 feet, drops 23,000 feet and covers some beautiful terrain.

The Western States 100 is one of four 100-mile running races that make up the Grand Slam of Ultrarunning. The other three events are the Vermont 100-mile Endurance Run, the Wasatch Front 100-mile Endurance Run in Utah and Colorado's Leadville Trail 100.

The Western States 100 evolved out of the Western States Trail Ride, a 100-mile endurance horseback riding event that began in 1955. In 1974, one of the riders, Gordy Ainsleigh, had a lame horse, so he decided to run the entire course and finished the event on foot in 23 hours and 47 minutes. In 1975, Ron Kelley ran the course along with the horses but dropped out at mile 97. In 1976, Ken Shirk became just the second runner to finish the course with the horses.

The first official Western States Endurance Run was held in 1977, and 14 runners showed up. They started with the horses on the Trail Ride, and 11 of them either dropped out or were pulled out by the organizers at the halfway point. Only one runner, Andy Gonzales, finished the race within the 24-hour time limit that was set for the riders

In 1978, 63 runners entered the Western States Endurance Run, and the race was held on a different day than the trail ride. In 1984, the Granite Chief Wilderness Area was established, and roughly four miles of the trail lay within its boundaries. There was debate over a large number of participants stampeding through this protected and pristine land. However, in 1988, the Western States Endurance Run and the Western States Trail Ride were given permission by Congress to continue with a limited field size.

The number of runners was capped at 369, the same size as the field in 1984. This limit made it necessary to implement a lottery system in order to determine who could race. A limited number of entries are awarded to winners of other races and to top-10 finishers of the previous Western States Endurance Run races, and the rest of the competitors are drawn randomly.

The event has become one of the most highly regarded ultrarunning races in the world. Ann Trason, who has won the race 14 times, holds the women's division course record of 17 hours, 37 minutes, 51 seconds. In 2004, Scott Jurek set a course record of 15 hours, 36 minutes, 27 seconds. However, in 2010, Geoff Roes broke that record with a finishing time of

15 hours, 7 minutes, 4 seconds. Also in 2010, Amy Palmeiro-Winters became the first amputee in history to complete the race and finished with a time of 27 hours, 43 minutes, 10 seconds.

Running Fast Fact

There are more than 250 running clubs and teams in the state of California.

Chapter Ten

Golden State Sun AND Snow

Skiing

Squaw Valley

Squaw Valley Ski Resort is located near beautiful Lake Tahoe. Wayne Poulsen and Alex Cushing were the original founders of the resort. However, shortly before the ski area opened in 1949, they parted ways and Cushing controlled the Squaw Valley Ski Corporation from that point until his death in 2006 at the age of 92.

Squaw Valley Ski Resort is one of the largest ski areas in the United States with over 4000 skiable acres, six peaks, 33 lifts, a 3.2-mile-long run, three terrain parks and a top elevation of over 9000 feet. The 1960 Winter Olympic Games were held there, and several alumni of the Squaw Valley Ski Team and Freestyle Team have gone on to compete in the Winter Olympic Games, including Tamara McKinney, Johnny Moseley, Julia Mancuso, Daron Rahlves, Shannon Bahrke, Marco Sullivan, Edith Thys and Bill Hudson.

Skiing Fast Fact

Skiing is big business in the Golden State, and California is home to 30 ski resorts.

Snowboarding

Shaun White

Shaun White was born in San Diego in 1986. He had two major surgeries to correct a heart defect before he was a year old, but fortunately that didn't prevent him from being active as a kid.

Despite living near the beach, his family made frequent trips to the mountains. And when Shaun was four, he was bombing down runs on skis and started snowboarding at age six. White entered his first amateur snowboard contest when he was just seven, landed a sponsorship deal from Burton that same year and turned pro at age 13.

Shaun won five national titles as an amateur and notched his first major win as a pro in 2001. At 16, he earned his first Winter X Games medal and has stood on a Winter X Games podium every year since.

Although White is best known for his exploits on snow, he's also a ripping skateboarder and has had some impressive accomplishments in that sport as well. White has been a professional skateboarder since he was 17 and has been mentored by skateboarding legend Tony Hawk since he was nine years old.

White has won 19 X Games medals so far in both skateboarding and snowboarding, and 11 of those medals are gold. In 2003, he became the first athlete to ever compete and medal in both the Summer and Winter X Games in two different sports.

In 2006, White became the first athlete to sweep the five-event U.S. Grand Prix series, which serves as an Olympic qualifier, and he went on to win a gold medal in Torino. Leading up to the 2010 Winter Olympics in Vancouver, one of his sponsors, Red Bull, created a special halfpipe for him to train on with the first-ever on-mountain foam pit. This Red Bull foam pit allowed Shaun to attempt tricks he never thought possible, including the first-ever back-to-back double cork.

White has had a sponsor since he was seven years old, and his corporate endorsement deals have included Burton Snowboards, Oakley, Birdhouse Skateboards, Park City Mountain Resort, Target Corporation, Red Bull, Ubisoft, Adio and Hewlett-Packard. White also has his own character on the game *Shaun Palmer's Pro Snowboarder* as well as the video game *Shaun White Snowboarding* and *Shaun White Skateboarding*. In 2009, *Forbes* magazine estimated that he had earned $9 million from his endorsement deals in 2008.

Medals

2003 Winter X Games—Gold (Superpipe)
2003 Winter X Games—Gold (Slopestyle)
2004 Winter X Games—Gold (Slopestyle)
2005 Winter X Games—Gold (Slopestyle)
2006 Winter X Games—Gold (Superpipe)
2006 Winter X Games—Gold (Slopestyle)
2006 Olympic Winter Games—Gold (Halfpipe)
2008 Winter X Games—Gold (Superpipe)
2009 Winter X Games—Gold (Superpipe)

2009 Winter X Games—Gold (Slopestyle)
2010 Winter X Games—Gold (Superpipe)
2010 Olympic Winter Games—Gold (Halfpipe)

Snowboarding Fast Fact

The first World Championship halfpipe competition was held in 1983 at Soda Springs. The founder of Sims Snowboards, Tom Sims, organized the event.

Chapter Eleven

But Wait, There's More!

Honorable Mentions

USOTC Chula Vista

The United States Olympic Training Center (USOTC) in Chula Vista sits on 150 acres at the base of Otay Lakes. The center, which opened in June 1995, is one of three in the nation—the other two are in Colorado Springs, Colorado, and Lake Placid, New York. The facility was a gift to the USOC from the San Diego National Sports Training Foundation, who raised the funds to build the center.

Olympics

The Games of the X Olympiad were hosted by Los Angeles in 1932. There were no other bids to host the Olympics that year, and because of the Great Depression, several nations and athletes were unable to afford to make the trip. Even the president of the United States at the time, Herbert Hoover, didn't show up, and he officially became the first head of government to not attend an Olympic Games being hosted by his own country.

The VIII Olympic Winter Games were hosted by Squaw Valley in 1960. Squaw Valley won the bid in 1955 and, at that time, had only one inhabitant and homeowner: Alexander Cushing, owner of the Squaw Valley Ski Resort. Many were shocked that a town with no mayor and a tiny resort with only one chairlift and a small lodge beat out St. Moritz, Switzerland; Garmisch-Partenkirchen, Germany; and Innsbruck, Austria, to secure the bid. Walt Disney was the Head of Pageantry for the 1960 Winter Games and reportedly put on quite a show.

This was also the first time that an Olympic Village was built to house all of the athletes, and these Games were the inspiration for the invention of "instant replay" by CBS. The invention was prompted by officials asking CBS to review videotape of the men's slalom race when they were unsure if a skier had missed a gate.

The Games of the XXIII Olympiad were again hosted by Los Angeles in 1984. As with the 1932 Olympic Games, Los Angeles was the only city that submitted a bid to host the Summer Olympics that year. This was largely because of the enormous debt that Montreal incurred from hosting the Games in 1976. The low level of interest in hosting the 1984 Games was certainly viewed as a significant threat to the future of the Olympics. Fortunately, Los Angeles was able to make the Games a financial success. As a result, other cities began to line up to host the Olympics once again.

Today, the Los Angeles and Montreal Games are used as examples for host cities of "how to" and "how not to" organize the Olympics. Montreal organizers had incurred skyrocketing debt eight years earlier by constructing new and costly venues, while the Los Angeles Organizing Committee utilized venues that were already in existence. In addition, 14 Eastern Bloc countries, including the Soviet Union, East Germany and Cuba, boycotted the 1984 Olympic Games.

Beach Volleyball

It's believed that beach volleyball was first played in 1915 at the Outrigger Canoe Club in Hawaii when there was no surf to be had. However, many regard 1920 as the true birth of the sport when the first beach volleyball courts were established in Santa Monica. Santa Monica is also credited with hosting the first professional beach volleyball tournament, the Olympia World Championship of Beach Volleyball, in 1976.

Today, the sport is played all around the world, has been an Olympic sport since 1996 and is popular in numerous coastal communities in California.

Quotable Californians

Baseball

"Baseball is like driving; it's the one who gets home safely that counts."
–Tommy Lasorda, Los Angeles Dodgers manager

"No matter how noble and special people want to make the playoffs out to be…it's a crapshoot."
–Orel Hershiser, former Dodger pitching ace

"My responsibility is to get my 25 guys playing for the name on the front of their uniform and not the one on the back."

–Tommy Lasorda

"Baseball is just my job."

–Barry Bonds, San Francisco Giants slugger

"I believe managing is like holding a dove in your hand. If you hold it too tightly you kill it, but if you hold it too loosely, you lose it."

–Tommy Lasorda

"When I hit it [number 500], I couldn't believe I hit it. Everything was in slow motion. It looked like it was stopped in midair. Then I saw it went past those people [on the left field wall] and I thought, 'Wow! I did it!'"

–Barry Bonds, on hitting his 500th career home run

"I bleed Dodger blue, and when I die, I'm going to the big Dodger in the sky."

–Tommy Lasorda

"I don't want to be on ESPN for the next 20 years."

–Russell Martin, on the possibility that Barry Bonds might hit homer number 755 against the Dodgers prior to a three-game Dodger–Giant series

"Guys ask me, don't I get burned out? How can you get burned out doing something you love? I ask you, have you ever got tired of kissing a pretty girl?"
–Tommy Lasorda, when questioned about his long career in the majors

"My history is San Francisco. That's my father, my godfather. Every friend in the world that I grew up with is there. There's no place in the world like San Francisco for me, right now. I don't know if there ever will be."

–Barry Bonds

"I'm in no way surprised by today's events. This is clearly a bad day for baseball and obviously a significant developmental milestone in a long-running steroid investigation. It's a tragic end to a fantastic career."
–Kevin V. Ryan, the former U.S. attorney who opened the BALCO probe in 2002, when it was announced that Barry Bonds would be indicted for lying under oath during his testimony in the BALCO case

"Say 'Dodgers' and people know you're talking about baseball. Say 'Braves' and they ask, 'What reservation?' Say 'Reds' and they think of communism. Say 'Padres' and they look around for a priest."

–Tommy Lasorda

Football

"There's no thrill like throwing a touchdown pass."
—Joe Montana, San Francisco 49ers quarterback

"I've been there and I've done that...I've never liked looking back, whether it's looking back at college or at high school. I'm going forward. I could do the analyst thing, but I would have to be gone every weekend, and I don't want that. I missed seeing my daughters grow up because of this crazy game."
—Joe Montana, on one of his reasons for retiring from the game

"Sports ideally teach discipline and commitment. They challenge you and build character for everything you do in life."
—Howie Long, Oakland Raiders

"Montana...looking, looking, throwing in the end zone...Clark caught it!"
—Vince Scully, calling the famous "Catch" by Dwight Clark in the 1982 NFC championship game between the San Francisco 49ers and the Dallas Cowboys

"To me, it was never about what I accomplished on the football field, it was about the way I played the game."
—Jerry Rice, former San Francisco 49ers wide receiver

"Winners, I am convinced, imagine their dreams first. They want it with all their heart and expect it to come true. There is, I believe, no other way to live."
—Joe Montana

"I feel like I'm the best, but you're not going to get me to say that."
—Jerry Rice

Basketball

"Some people are going to have to grow some tough skin they hadn't had to grow before. Pat is a direct guy. That's going to really be different than everyone is used to. And he's going to say it in a way they're not used to a coach saying it and right in their face…He just wants you to play the game the right way."
—Magic Johnson, on former Lakers coach Pat Riley

"I miss all the police officers. I miss all the valet parkers at the mall. I miss all the little people. I miss everybody."
—Shaquille O'Neal, when asked by a reporter if he missed his fans in Los Angeles

"When he found out he had Parkinson's, he showed such great courage by appearing in public no matter what. Because of Muhammad, I've been trying to do the same thing ever since I found out I was HIV positive."
—Magic Johnson, on his hero Muhammad Ali

"I don't want to be the next Michael Jordan, I only want to be Kobe Bryant."
—Kobe Bryant, Los Angeles Lakers

"The important thing is this, just because I'm doing well doesn't mean that they're going to do well if they get HIV. A lot of people have died since I have announced. This disease is not going anywhere."
—Magic Johnson

"In the seven or eight years we were together, we were never together."
—Shaquille O'Neal, on Lakers teammate Kobe Bryant

"Everybody on a championship team doesn't get publicity, but everyone can say he's a champion."
—Magic Johnson

"I don't think there will ever be another 6-foot-9 point guard who smiles while he humiliates you."
—James Worthy, on longtime Lakers teammate Magic Johnson

"It was the first game ever called on account of hugs."
—Magic Johnson, who received a warm welcome from fellow players when he returned from retirement to score 25 points and win the MVP award at the 1992 All-Star Game

"Each warrior wants to leave the mark of his will, his signature, on the important acts he touches. This is not the voice of ego but of the human spirit, rising up and declaring that it has something to contribute. In every contest, there comes a moment that separates winning from losing. The true warrior understands and seizes that moment by giving an effort so intense and so intuitive that it could only be called one from the heart."
–Pat Riley, Lakers head coach

"Incense. Books. Just weird."
–Shaquille O'Neal, when asked how Phil Jackson's coaching style is different from those of other coaches

"With all of you men out there who think that having a thousand different ladies is pretty cool, I have learned in my life I've found out that having one woman a thousand different times is much more satisfying."
–Wilt Chamberlain, Los Angeles Lakers

"If you've got a Corvette that runs into a brick wall, you know what's going to happen. He's a Corvette. I'm a brick wall."
–Shaquille O'Neal, when asked how he might react if Kobe comes barreling down the lane in the Heat–Lakers game

Hockey

"[There's] nothing better than playing in a rink where the fans are loud and making a bunch of noise.

It makes it a more exciting, more intense game, one you like to be part of. How do we know until we get there [how things will be]? I'm optimistic that hopefully [the fans] will be able to forget about the dark days we put them through for a whole year and come back and enjoy it."
—Scott Niedermayer, Anaheim Ducks

"In selecting the name the Anaheim Ducks, we are respecting the heritage of a tremendous organization that has been a very important and visible part of the community, not to mention Western Conference champions and a Stanley Cup finalist."
—Henry Samueli, owner of the Anaheim Ducks, on changing the name of the franchise after purchasing it from the Disney Corporation

"Anaheim Ducks feels great. The Ducks were part of the original name. Maybe the 'Mighty' was more about the Disney side of it."
—Teemu Selanne, Anaheim Ducks forward, on his team's new name

"Dustin [Brown] is projected to start the season in Los Angeles. We are obviously pleased to have him signed and under contract with our organization. We think he has a real bright future with the Kings."
—Dave Taylor, Los Angeles Kings general manager, on Dustin Brown

"My goal is still to be a number one goalie, and I think it's going to happen next season [either in San Jose or elsewhere]. I'm really counting on that. And I think I made the smart decision to sign with the Sharks."
 —Vesa Toskala, former San Jose Sharks goaltender

"Procrastination is one of the most common and deadliest of diseases, and its toll on success and happiness is heavy."
 —Wayne Gretzky, former Los Angeles Kings forward

"Finally, there was that one day when Peter called me and said, 'Bruce, if you're really serious about Gretzky, let's talk.' I was stunned. I didn't know what to say. I was like, 'Oookay.' I mumbled and bumbled around. I said, 'Well, what's up?' And he said, 'Well, first of all, you could trade me the entire franchise, the entire team, and it wouldn't be enough for Gretzky. But I need cash.' So I said, 'OK…Let's talk.' And that's how it began."
 —Bruce McNall, former owner of the Los Angeles Kings

"Over the next couple of weeks, I finally got it through my head that assets do depreciate. To reload the team with fresh blood and $15 million US, which at that time was $18-and-a-half million Canadian, to a small-market team was a lot of money. I phoned Bruce [McNall] back and said, 'Bruce, I think we can put something together.'"
 —Peter Pocklington, Edmonton Oilers owner, on his reasons for trading Gretzky

"I was so scared. I remember telling Janet, 'Wow, this is not as easy or going to be as easy as people anticipate.' It was frightening to me. I was playing on a team that had finished 20th out of 21 teams the year before."
–Wayne Gretzky, on his initial feelings about being traded to the Los Angeles Kings

"The Canadians are up in arms! Quick, call out the Mounties!"
–Los Angeles area local newscaster on Canada's reaction to the Gretzky trade

California Sports Quiz

Questions

1. What's the longest the Giants franchise has gone between World Series titles?
   a) 33 years
   b) 40 years
   c) 48 years
   d) 56 years

2. What is the name of the stadium where the Los Angeles Dodgers call home?
   a) Ebbets Field
   b) Los Angeles Memorial Coliseum
   c) Western Park
   d) Dodger Stadium

3. What year did the Dodgers last win the World Series?
   a) 1984
   b) 1986
   c) 1988
   d) 1990

4. How many Super Bowl Championships have the San Francisco 49ers won?
   a) Two
   b) Four
   c) Five
   d) Seven

5. How many confirmed fatal shark attacks have there been in California waters since 1950?
   a) 12
   b) 19
   c) 26
   d) 33

Answers to California Sports Quiz on Page 205.

Hall of Fame Californians

California Sports Hall of Fame

Christian Okoye, former All-Pro running back for the Kansas City Chiefs, founded the California Sports Hall of Fame. With support from some of the biggest names in sports from the state of California, this influential organization was formed to honor our sports heroes, support struggling athletes, highlight California sports history and, more importantly, promote education through sport.

Baseball

- Steve Garvey
- Reggie Jackson
- Willie Mays
- Jackie Robinson
- Dave Winfield

Basketball

- Elgin Baylor
- Wilt Chamberlain
- Ann Meyers Drysdale
- Earvin "Magic" Johnson
- Cheryl Miller
- Bill Walton
- Jerry West

Football

- Marcus Allen
- Fred Biletnikoff
- Eric Dickerson

- Dan Fouts
- Rosey Grier
- Deacon Jones
- Merlin Olsen
- Jim Otto
- Jim Plunkett
- Kellen Winslow

Coaches

- Tom Flores
- Tommy Lasorda
- Bill Walsh
- John Wooden

Tennis

- Billy Jean King

Track and Field

- Rafer Johnson
- Jackie Joyner-Kersee
- Bob Mathias
- Mike Powell
- Donald Quarrie
- Dwight Stone

California Sports Quiz Answers

1. d) The New York Giants won the World Series in 1954, and the franchise didn't break its long-standing San Francisco curse until 2010.

2. d) The Los Angeles Dodgers have been playing at Dodger Stadium since 1962.

3. c) In the all-California World Series, the Dodgers defeated the Oakland Athletics in five games to win their fifth World Series titles.

4. c) Since joining the NFL in 1946, the 49ers have won five Super Bowl Championships.

5. a) There have been 12 confirmed fatal shark attacks in California waters since 1950.

Notes on Sources

Books

Colvin, Geoff. *Talent is Overrated*. New York, NY: Penguin Group, 2008.

Web Sources

basketball-reference.com
ESPN.com
golflink.com
imdb.com
nba.com
profootballhof.com
surfline.com
USATODAY.com
usaswimming.com
USOC.org
usta.com
wikipedia.org

Raul Guisado lives in Northern California, where he works as a sports performance coach for athletes at the NCAA, Olympic and professional levels. He was the World Cup and Olympic coach for the U.S. ski team from 1995 to 1998 and has coached athletes who have competed in the last four Winter Olympic Games. In addition to co-authoring a surf travel guide, he has written two books, *The Art of Surfing* and *Cross-Training for Endurance Athletes*. He lives with his wife, Kendra, and son, Dylan.

J. Alexander Poulton is a writer, photographer and genuine sports enthusiast. He's even willing to admit he has "called in sick" during the broadcasts of major sports events so that he can get in as much viewing as possible.

He has earned a BA in English literature and a graduate diploma in journalism, and has over 20 sports books to his credit, including books on hockey, soccer, golf and the Olympics.